PASSPORT
TO CORNWALL

Phil Billington

ISBN 978-0957646162

Published by
Polperro Heritage Press
Clifton-upon-Teme
Worcestershire
WR6 6DH, UK
www.polperropress.co.uk

Printed by Orphans Press
Leominster HR6 0LD
United Kingdom

KERNOW<KERNOW~KERNOW>KERNOW
CORNWALL<CORNWALL>CORNWALL

Kernow a'gas Dynnergh ~ Onen hag Oll
Welcome to Cornwall ~ One and All

PASSPORT
NOTICE

THIS DOCUMENTATION INVALID OUTSIDE
KERNOW/CORNWALL & THE ISLES OF SCILLY

THIS IS NOT A SUBSTITUTE
FOR A HOME OFFICE OR
STANNARY PARLIAMENT PASSPORT

LEGAL BEARER HAS RIGHT OF SAFE PASSAGE WITHIN
KERNOW/CORNWALL & THE ISLES OF SCILLY

Do **not** remove or deface this page

KERNOW<KERNOW~KERNOW>KERNOW
CORNWALL<CORNWALL>CORNWALL

KERNOW<KERNOW~KERNOW>KERNOW
CORNWALL<CORNWALL>CORNWALL

PASSPORT
TERMS & CONDITIONS

(i) Do not remove or deface bespoke pages.

(ii) This biometrically secure passport is invalid outside Kernow/ Cornwall and the Isles of Scilly. Cornish language use mostly follows Standard Written Form.

(iii) This is not a substitute for a passport as issued by the UK Home Office or the Cornish Stannary Parliament. Legal bearer has right of safe passage within Kernow/Cornwall/Isles of Scilly. Future travel may necessitate visa documentation.

(iv) This passport book must be produced when requested by an official or if required to be stamped. Recipient under no obligation to necessitate stamping. Official stickers are deemed an acceptable substitute to stamping.

(v) It is admissible to make brief personal notes within bespoke blank pages but not to deface any stampings/official writings therein. Guidebook for information only and responsibility cannot be accepted for any omissions, errors or inaccuracies within. Annotation permitted.

(vi) This passport book to be kept safe and secure at all times. Signature bearer deemed legally responsible. Non-transferable. Passport invalid if not completed. Misuse may result in confiscation and possible legal proceedings.

(vii) Copyright control exists throughout. Copies deemed criminally invalid.

(viii) Signature signifies acceptance of all terms and conditions.

(ix) Non of the above affect signature bearer's statutory rights.

KERNOW<KERNOW~KERNOW>KERNOW
CORNWALL<CORNWALL>CORNWALL

PASSPORT PROFILE FORM

COMPLETE FULLY TO LEGALLY VALIDATE

(i) Surname ---

(ii) Given First Name(s) ---

(iii) Nationality --

(iv) Date of Birth -------- Day ------------ Month ------------- Year

(v) Gender --

(vi) Place of Birth ---

> *Affix Valid*
>
> *Passport*
>
> *Photo*

(vii) Bearer's Signature ------------------------------- Date ------------

Do not remove or deface this page ~ Copies criminally invalid ~ Non-transferable

FURVLEN BROFIL TREMENGUMMYAS ~ PASSPORT PROFILE FORM

PASSPORT STAMP PAGES

- *The following blank pages are for stamping (small stickers acceptable) at participating centres, attractions, events, activities, museums, hotels, B&B's, shops, pubs, restaurants etc.*

- *It is admissible to make brief personal notes within pages but not to deface title page nor any stampings/official writings.*

- *This passport book must be produced when requested by an official or if required to be stamped. Recipient under no obligation to necessitate stamping. Official stickers are deemed an acceptable substitute to stamping.*

Do **not** remove or deface this page

FOLENNOW STAMPYS TREMENGUMMYAS

Do not remove or deface this page

Myghternedh Kernow
(Kingdom of Cornwall)

<<<<<<<<<<<PASSPORT STAMP PAGES>>>>>>>>>>>

FOLENNOW STAMPYS TREMENGUMMYAS

Do not remove or deface this page

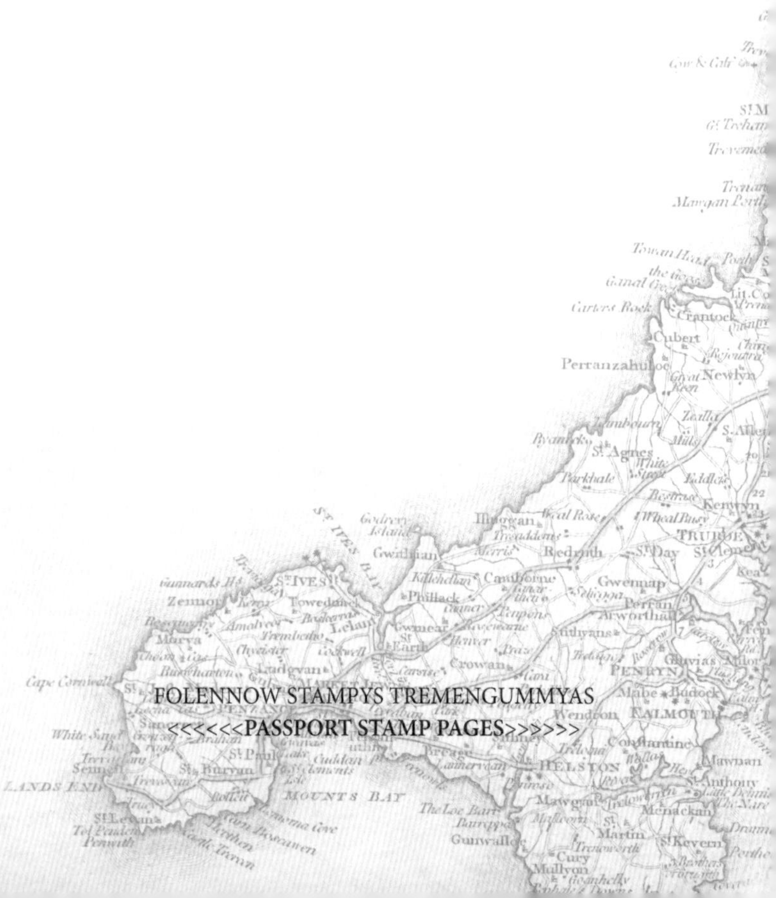

FOLENNOW STAMPYS TREMENGUMMYAS

<<<<<<PASSPORT STAMP PAGES>>>>>>>

<<<<<<<<<<PASSPORT STAMP PAGES>>>>>>>>>>
FOLENNOW STAMPYS TREMENGUMMYAS
Do not remove or deface this page

FOLENNOW STAMPYS TREMENGUMMYAS
<<<<<<PASSPORT STAMP PAGES>>>>>>

<<<<<<<<<<PASSPORT STAMP PAGES>>>>>>>>>>
FOLENNOW STAMPYS TREMENGUMMYAS
Do not remove or deface this page

FOLENNOW STAMPYS TREMENGUMMYAS
<<<<<<PASSPORT STAMP PAGES>>>>>>

<<<<<<<<<PASSPORT STAMP PAGES>>>>>>>>>
FOLENNOW STAMPYS TREMENGUMMYAS
Do not remove or deface this page

FOLENNOW STAMPYS TREMENGUMMYAS
<<<<<<PASSPORT STAMP PAGES>>>>>>

<<<<<<<<<<PASSPORT STAMP PAGES>>>>>>>>>>
FOLENNOW STAMPYS TREMENGUMMYAS
Do not remove or deface this page

**END OF PASSPORT
STAMP PAGES**

GUIDEBOOK

For information only ~ Annotation permitted

• *In this Standard English Language version of 'Passport To Cornwall' the guidebook consists of general information the traveller to Cornwall may find helpful, giving wide-ranging insight to the area and suggestions for places to see. Responsibility cannot be accepted for any omissions, errors or inaccuracies within. These are not complete listings and visits to Tourist Information Centres are highly recommended, especially as their help and advice is both impartial and free.*

• *Expect to be charged entry for various attractions, events, activities etc although there are many things that are totally free to enjoy. This includes thousands of acres of areas of outstanding natural beauty, mile upon mile of stunning views, magnificent walks, award winning beaches, over 400 miles of coastline, more than any other UK region and so much more besides.*

• *For ease of use Cornwall has been split into two broad areas, namely North and South, mainly concentrating on coastal locations. Other places further inland have been listed following on from their nearest main coastal settlement. North and South Cornwall are defined here by a line drawn through Launceston, Bodmin, Camborne and Land's End. These places have been included in the North Cornwall section, as have the Isles of Scilly.*

Cornwall is consistently voted the best UK holiday destination and is indeed a fantastic land, conjuring up images of miners, smugglers and wreckers. Thoughts of pasties and cream teas intermingle with stories of King Arthur, Poldark and those of Daphne du Maurier. Iconic Cornish destinations bring to mind rugged Land's End, mystical Tintagel Castle, historic St Michael's Mount and the Eden Project but there's so much more. Cornwall is an entrancing land of unique beauty, magical charm, warmth, tranquillity, mystery and heritage.

Mother nature in general and waves and storms in particular have battered Cornwall for millennia, molding and shaping the land into what it is today, a place of incredible beauty. Emotions cannot help but stir whenever Cornwall's name is mentioned. Steeped in folk-law, Celtic soul and tradition, Cornwall evokes the essence of an ancient, yet proud and resilient living culture. One and all are more than welcome and as Cornwall is nature's paradise, disappointment is not an option. Once visited it stays in the heart and like every turn of the tide the need to return again is both compulsive and inevitable. Find time to escape and explore Cornwall, the delectable Duchy, it's just so fabulously brilliant!

These guidebook notes offer a wealth of information for the traveller to Cornwall, so do enjoy dipping into them whenever visiting this evocotive and unforgettable land. As of 2014 the Cornish people themselves are proudly and legally recognised as a nation, having gained distinctive national minority status within the federation of EU nations. This entitles them to the same rights, protection and recognition of language, history and culture as other British national Celtic minorities and this historic event ultimately resulted in the issuing of this passport documentation.

Kernow a'gas Dynnergh ~ Onen hag Oll
(Welcome to Cornwall ~ One and All)

CONTENTS

Key Information

General Interest

A Taste of Cornwall

North Cornwall

South Cornwall

Key Information

BORDER CONTROL

The Cornish for passport is *tremengummyas*. Make sure a valid passport is held before travelling. Identity cards for British Citizens are no longer a legal form of identification. Cornwall is surrounded by sea apart from its landlocked border with Devon, England, which is defined in most part by the River Tamar (Dowr Tamer). All border crossing checkpoints are currently open with key positions located on the A39 Atlantic Highway, the A30 Great South West Road and the A38 Expressway. An outbound toll is payable between the A38 border for road vehicles at the Saltash crossing, adjacent to the Royal Albert Railway Bridge. Proof of vehicle ownership, insurance and a valid driving licence may be required to be shown at border crossings and/or on route within Cornwall. Visitors to Cornwall are subject to United Kingdom law. Passport control is operational at various designated sites including Newquay Airport and ports such as Penzance and Falmouth. In Cornwall cars are driven on the left-hand side of the road and the minimum age for purchasing alcohol is 18. Smoking is restricted to those over 16 and gambling is legal at the age of 18 (National Lottery 16). Due to potential Border Control policy changes future travel within Cornwall may necessitate further documentation in the form of a valid entry visa. At Border Control and elsewhere, close circuit television (CCTV) is operational 24 hours a day. For security and safety management reasons always be vigilant, never leave luggage or any other personal belongings unattended and be prepared to have them searched by staff if so requested.

CURRENCY

In the Cornish language money is *mona*. The designated currency unit used within Cornwall is decimal pounds sterling (£GBP) and within the coinage 100 pence (p) = £1. Bank note units consist of £5, £10, £20 and £50. Denominations of coinage are 1p, 2p, 5p, 10p, 20p, 50p, £1 and £2. The Cornish Stannary Parliament, the Seneth an

Stenegow Kernow, issued its own currency in 1974 and 1985 but at present this is not legal tender. The notes, including the millennium year 2000 issue of the 500 Dynar note, are highly prized collectors' items and their current worth far exceeds their face value, as do old mining companies 'coinage' trade tokens.

LANGUAGE

In Cornish, the word for the Cornish language is *Kernowek* and similarly Cornwall is *Kernow*. English is presently the dominant language within Cornwall, with the Cornish language being currently understood and spoken by a minority of the population but renewed interest has meant more youngsters are being encouraged to learn the language both in school and at home, with adult classes also flourishing. Books written in Cornish are increasingly common and the Cornish Language Fellowship, the Kowethas an Yeth Kernewek, is dedicated to the promotion of this ancient Celtic Brythonic language. Although Cornish is not as commonly spoken nowadays, the written word is evident in many places, often with signage written in both Cornish and English. The strong, distinctive Cornish accent speaks volumes about this fiercely independent thinking region but don't mistake dialect for the actual Cornish language. One of the last females to speak Cornish as a natural, fluent tongue was Dolly Pentreath of Mousehole who died in 1777 at the ripe old age of 102. Zennor attests the male claim through John Davey who died in 1891. However both of these also spoke English and it's claimed therefore that the last person who only spoke Cornish was monoglot Chesten Marchant who died in 1676 at Gwithian.

By 1800 the spread of English had finally taken its toll when Cornish as a community language stopped being spoken completely but in 2002 Cornish was finally recognised by the government as an official UK minority language. In 2008 various stems of Kernowek were brought together resulting in the Standard Written Form (SWF) of the language being ultimately ratified. Various phrase books, dictionaries and language courses mean that brushing up on the basics before a holiday is both easy and highly recommended. Throughout this book are helpful Cornish words. Some useful ones to start off with are: *ea* (yes), *na* (no), *mar plek* (please), *meur ras* (thank you), *hou/dydh da* (hello) and *duw genes* (goodbye). Within Cornwall the language is reflected through some unusual place names such as Praze-an-Beeble, Egloshayle, Menheniot, Tywardreath, Ponsanooth and Zennor, to name but a few. There are also many places named after various rather obscure saints such as St Endellion, St Erth, St Keverne and St Veep.

TOURIST INFORMATION CENTRES

Tourist Information Centres are a must to visit, as their local knowledge is invaluable. They are a treasure-trove of information and full of helpful leaflets (many free), books, maps, advice, ideas and suggestions on all sorts of local attractions, events, activities, places to eat, travel, transport and so much more. Many of the staff work on a voluntary basis and some even offer free (or low cost) guided walks around their area. Local accommodation can usually be arranged although advanced booking is always advised. Cornwall is getting more popular than ever and has millions of visitors annually. Tourist Information Centres may well describe Cornwall as the Delectable Duchy, which it certainly is, with over 25% designated as an area of outstanding natural beauty. Over 40% of the Cornish coastline is National Trust owned, which is a breathtaking achievement.

EMERGENCY SERVICES

In the case of an emergency response situation, stay calm and phone 999 (free). Be ready to state your name, location and the reason for the call. Ask clearly for police, fire brigade, ambulance or other emergency services such as the coastguard and lifeboat, which are also available to contact by phoning 112 (free). To contact the police when it's less urgent than 999 phone 101 (charge). This service can be used to report crimes that have already happened, for general police advice or to raise local policing. If urgent medical help is required for non life-threatening symptoms and is needed fast but not for an emergency call, then ring 111 (free) to contact NHS111, which is a confidential 24-hour health information and advice helpline, which also provides access to non-urgent local healthcare facilities. It is also possible to visit the Accident & Emergency (A&E) department of a local hospital or book an appointment with a local doctor/ general practitioner (GP) as a temporary patient. The Maritime & Coastguard Agency (MCA), formally the HM Coastguard Search & Rescue service, co-ordinate sea, cliff and shoreline emergency response and are based at Newquay Airport. They perform an amazing job, as does the lifeboat service, the Royal National Lifeboat Institute (RNLI). The invaluable National Coastwatch Institute (NCI) also provides a dedicated and fully trained voluntary service, established in 1994 following many Coastguard station closures.

General Interest

CLIMATE

The Cornish for sunny is *howlyek* and fine weather is *kewer vas*. Cornwall has a mild, marine climate thus making it an ideal holiday destination, in fact it has the mildest and sunniest weather on mainland Britain. Winter is short, spring early, summer is long and autumn doesn't know when to stop. Snow is a rarity on the coast as are days of frost; May is usually the sunniest month. As Cornwall is almost completely surrounded by sea the influence of the Gulf Stream on its long coastline gives it a unique British climate. The rugged north Cornish coastline faces the direct fury of the Celtic Sea area of the Atlantic Ocean, whilst the south 'Cornish Riviera' coast is far more sheltered with the British Sea (English Channel) caressing its shoreline. The Cornish palm thrives in the mild climate giving the area a distinct Mediterranean feel.

EARLY HISTORY

The history of Cornwall (Kernow) is a long, rich tapestry of events. The sea has been arguably as important, if not more so than the land, in shaping the very character of Cornwall, with fishing and mining once being at its very heart. Cornwall contains more ancient monuments that any other area of Great Britain. It's full of many types of wonderful ancient stone constructions such as hole stones, standing circles, inscribed stones and burial chambers, around which have developed many myths and legends. There is also a wealth of old castles and hill forts in various states of decay and repair. Many tourists suppose Cornwall is literally named after an ancient boundary wall of corn but this concept is obviously incorrect and in fact the River Tamar defines the boundary. The prefix Corn maybe derived from the Roman Cornovii meaning Celtic hill dwellers, perhaps from the Celtic *cern* (kern) meaning horn, or even from the Latin cornu meaning a peninsular, a horn of land. The suffix wall may stem from *waelas* meaning strangers or perhaps *walh* meaning Briton. So Cornwall literally means the

'Celtic peninsular hill dwelling strangers of Briton'. It's also been known in the past as West Wales, Belerion and part of Dumnonia.

The Cornovii (Kernyw) tribe inhabited a remote horn of land in ancient Celtic Dumnonia. Their indigenous language developed into what is now referred to as Cornish (Kernowek). Their land, nowadays known as Cornwall or Kernow, was rich in deposits of both tin and copper, metals vital in the manufacture of bronze and trading became extensive. Gold, silver, zinc and lead were also present. When the Romans, Vikings and Anglo-Saxons invaded Britain their authority on the Celtic Cornovii was minimal as it was still ruled by its own Cornish kings such as the early sixth century King Margh (Mark) and the ninth century King Donyarth. In Latin this independent kingdom was named Cornubia. Skirmishes were inevitable and in AD 936 the east bank of the River Tamar was chosen by Athelstan, the then Saxon king of England, as the boundary between Wessex (England) and what was left of the neighbouring ancient Celtic land of Dumnonia, namely the horn of land belonging to the Cornovii, which was known to the Saxon's as Cornweal. Most of Celtic Dumnonia had been sadly lost and subsequently absorbed into Saxon West Wessex, which today forms the English counties of Somerset and Devon.

The distinct Celtic Kingdom of Kernow became officially isolated on the Cornweal (Cornwall) peninsular and was considered a foreign land, as indeed were Wales, Scotland and Ireland. At the start of the Norman Conquest (1066) William the Conqueror made Cadoc (Kadog), a direct descendant of the royal line of Cornwall, the Earl of Cornwall but soon Celtic-speaking Normans handpicked by the King stood in as assertive caretaker earls and viceroys of Cornwall. The Celtic nation looked on the apparently benign Normans as allies against their common Anglo-Saxon foe, as indeed they had with the Vikings. The Domesday Book (1086) recorded the fact that landowners in Cornwall held their land from the Earl of Cornwall and not from the King of England. In 1086 the Earl of Cornwall was Robert, Count of Mortaigne, who had been granted the title by his half brother William the Conqueror (William I of England). Robert was in effect King William's ambassadorial viceroy, in short a diplomatic and influential representative of England within the client country of Cornwall. Edward III created the Duchy of Cornwall estate for his son Edward, the Black Prince in 1337. Tragically, through the centuries many Cornish lives were lost in various riots and altercations over such things as taxes (as in the 1497 uprising), prayer books and corn. War and disease also took a heavy toll. The 1508 Charter of Pardon was granted to Cornwall by Henry VII and stated that no new laws should be passed without the backing of the Cornish Stannary Parliament (Seneth an Stenegow Kernow) and the people of Cornwall. This indeed confirmed and strengthened Cornwall as an influential nation.

NATIONAL FLAG & COAT OF ARMS

The flag of St Piran can be found all over Cornwall, on land as well as sea. It consists of a white cross on a black background. This is said to represent St Piran's triumph of good over evil, from darkness into light, or indeed the molten white tin he noticed flowing from dark rock (cassiterite tin ore) within his sooty hearth when the stone heated up; hence why Piran is the patron saint of Cornish miners. The flag has ancient origins but its first known written reference as a standard (heraldic flag) representing Cornwall was in 1838 by Cornishman Davies Gilbert, who described it as the former banner of St Piran and the Standard of Cornwall. The flag has become symbolic of Cornish pride and independence, being proudly flown throughout the Duchy. St Piran's Day is eagerly celebrated every 5th March and there is hope it will soon become a Cornish bank holiday. Cornwall has its own national coat of arms, an emblem that includes a sea fisherman (see 13), a tin miner (see 11) and a bird, the Cornish chough (see 16). Within a shield depicting the waves of the sea are 15 gold circles on a black inner shield. These are now thought to possibly represent gold raised in 1239 by Richard Earl/ Duke of Cornwall and by the Cornish people themselves as ransom payment for prisoners held by the Saracens during the Crusades. A scroll at the base of the coat of arms bears the ancient Duchy motto 'One and All', possibly referring to the raising of that ransom by the generous Cornish, although some believe it to be the translation for an old Cornish battle cry or maybe the pact between smugglers and their local community.

NATIONAL ANTHEM

Written around 1824-1825, the Reverend Stephen Hawker composed the *Song of the Western Men*, which is now used as the unofficial Cornish National Anthem of unity, better known today as 'Trelawny'. It's enthusiastically sung to the tune of the Welsh national anthem *Land of My Fathers* and as often as possible. It's based on the story of the Protestant religious hero Jonathan Trelawny, a Cornish bishop who with others didn't die in 1688 at the hands of the Catholic King James II but actually died in 1721. Another Cornish anthem is *Bro Goth Agan Tasow* (*Old Land of Our Fathers*). It was written by the avid Cornish language revivalist and proud Cornishman Henry Jenner and is also keenly sung to the tune *Land of My Fathers*.

NATIONAL TARTAN

The Cornish are a Celtic nation like the Scots and as such both are entitled to wear tartan woven cloth. The colours of the Cornish national tartan all have significance, the black and white represents St Piran's cross and the national flag of Cornwall (see 8), the blue is for the sea that surrounds the Cornish coast, the gold represents old Cornish kings and gold coins (see 8) and the red is for the colour of the beak and legs of Cornwall's national bird, the chough (see 16). There is a hunting tartan, which has all the colours of the national tartan but with the addition of green, which the old Cornish wrestlers traditionally wore. Also there is a St Piran's dress kilt, which is predominantly black and white but also includes a little chough red and wrestling green woven in it. In Cornwall kilts seem to be mostly worn for formal occasions along with special kilt pins, a sporran, a ceremonial small knife, a belt buckle, a waistcoat and a jacket.

MINING

Cornwall is geologically interesting and many valuable ores and minerals have been found and subsequently mined in the area. Granite intrusions are the reason for this wealth of riches and their weathered decay the source of china clay, another very important resource. Tin, copper, lead, silver, gold etc. have all been worked by skilled Cornish miners and many of the long since deserted mine shafts have gravestone-like chimneys with derelict engine houses standing guard over their remains. The dangers that miners faced were daunting and some paid the ultimate price with their own life. At one time half the world's tin was produced in Cornwall until cheaper imports resulted in the inevitable decline of the industry, as was the case with other such metals. This resulted in many miners leaving Cornwall to seek similar employment abroad in such places as Australia and America, where they were known as Cousin Jacks. A sad ending indeed for such a proud and brave heritage, although with the ever-increasing price of tin some mines may well be considered viable once again. Exceptionally valuable deposits of the rare element indium have recently been discovered at South Crofty mine near Redruth, together with significant new tin and copper veins and these may well create a resurgence in the fortunes of the Cornish mining industry.

Over the years many a miner died through contracting debilitating lung diseases such as silicosis, tuberculosis and bronchitis. Their quest to procure the valuable ores associated with local granite intrusions came at a high price. The damp, hot, dusty and smoky conditions they endured underground greatly reduced their life expectancy and arthritis was common. It was a very physically demanding job and fatigue during long shifts in a poor working environment, together with poor living conditions such as overcrowding, lack of basic sanitation, poverty and malutrition, all conspired to work against them. The romantic concept of being a Cornish miner was, in reality, far from ideal. Death was a daily threat and the unseen dangers were as big a killer as the obvious ones, perhaps even more so. Women also worked at the mines but always above ground. They were referred to as bal maidens, *bal* being Cornish for mine and would have worked very long, back-breaking shifts of about ten hours daily, six days a week, with only Sundays off. Nowadays heritage mining areas, even if devoid of any mining activity, are major tourist attractions and have evolved into a highly fascinating and profitable industry.

CHINA CLAY

The industrial volcanic-like cones of white china clay spoil tips which can be seen for miles around the St Austell area resemble the snow-topped mountain peaks of the Swiss Alps, although many have now been thoughtfully landscaped. The Chinese mountain of Kao Ling was the original site of the discovery of kaolin, a clay mineral resulting from the weathering of feldspar, a constituent of granite, which was then used in the oriental manufacture of porcelain. Devon born William Fox Cookworthy first discovered kaolin (china clay) in Cornwall and also thought up how to manufacture porcelain without importing it. He found the kaolin in 1746 at Tregonning Hill near Helston, where it was locally known as moorstone, a type of weathered, decayed granite, once thought to be virtually useless.

FISHING

Cornwall had many great fishing centres in the past, the industry being the mainstay of many a family. Pilchard (*Clupea pilchardus*) was the name the Cornish gave to a large sardine, or indeed a small herring. They were also known as Cornish ducks or fair-maids. The old Cornish word for pilchard was *pilseir* and in medieval times it was written as pilcher. Nowadays just referring to the fish as 'Cornish' gives them special value, although shoal numbers are nowhere the size they used to be. With the rebranding of the pilchard, the EU has actually given the term 'Cornish sardine' its blessing and honoured it with protected status, as long as it's caught within six miles of the Cornish coastline and landed and processed on Cornish soil. Together with the 'Cornish' pasty (see 22), it's now not only protected by name but also revered worldwide. The pilchard was considered to be the king of fish and the old saying 'pilchards are food, money and light, all in one night' really did ring true. Around Cornish harbours hung the rich smell of fish as the pilchards were gutted, pressed for their valuable oil and salted fresh from the nets. Lookout towers or huts were specially built to spot large shoals of pilchards when they came close to shore to feed. These towers were known as huers' huts (*huer* means shout) and when the fish were sighted a cry of hevva (meaning shoal of fish found) was called, hence the phrase hue and cry. Boats were guided to the 'liquid silver' shoals by means of the huer's signals in the hope that the cast nets would bag a substantial catch. In celebration women would bake hevva cakes (see 30). There are still a few fishing fleets based in Cornwall these days, with Newlyn being the largest but they are just a shadow of the industry that once proudly flourished.

WRECKERS

In an age long gone it was said that unscrupulous souls would try to lure ships onto rocks with the aid of lanterns, in order to wreck them and plunder the cargo. Some dismiss this as mere fantasy, fit only for books and films, whilst others believe it a reality. The facts are lost in the mists of time but it's true to say that villagers took a very keen interest in any ships found floundering on the rocks or washed up on the shore and indeed they were considered fair game. Any crew left alive were hopefully rescued and the vessel then picked clean but legally back then a 'wreck of the sea' had to first meet the condition that no living creature from it ever reached shore. Customs officials known as preventative men tried to police this activity but often arrived after the deed had been done. Many Cornish graveyards bear witness to the great loss of human life the sea has caused. The wrecks of once noble ships litter the coastal waters of Cornwall and some can still be seen wedged between the jaws of merciless rocks.

SMUGGLERS

In days of old Cornwall was renowned for its enterprising smuggling and many considered the smugglers themselves to be heroes. The Cornish coast path was well trodden by government officials on the look out for anyone trying to evade import duties. Illicit tobacco, brandy, gin, rum, silk, tea and other such luxuries flooded into Cornish harbours, coves and secret places, to be stored in caves, tunnels, cellars, under floorboards or anywhere else that the excise men hopefully couldn't find. Profit was the name of the game but a certain amount of notoriety and smugness crept in, especially for those that stayed undetected from the authorities and at large to perpetuate such crimes. Smuggling was known as free trade and the free traders ran the risk of fines, imprisonment or even hanging if they were caught. Sometimes the preventative men and even upstanding members of the community turned a blind eye and in return took a share of the spoils.

CORNISH CHOUGH

The charismatic Cornish red-billed chough (pronounced chuff) has the Latin name *Pyrrhocorax pyrrhocorax* meaning fire or flame-coloured raven. It's Cornwall's national bird and in Cornish its name is *palores*, meaning digger. They are sometimes known as chows after their piercing 'che-ow' sounding call and feed mainly on insects, invertebrates and sometimes fallen grain and berries. Their preferred habitat is coastal rocky cliffs, sea-caves, headlands, short grazed grassland and heathland. It's a black member of the crow family with distinctive red legs and downward curved red bill. They are highly acrobatic when in flight and a group of choughs is collectively known as a chatter (or clatter). Legend has it that the soul of King Arthur went into the chough and his blood is what colours its beak and legs. They were often blamed for stealing shiny objects such as money and, because of their red colouring, were often associated with the cause of fires. Over the centuries their numbers gradually declined to the point of extinction in 1973 due to such things as trapping, shooting, poisoning, egg-collecting, taxidermy and loss of habitat due to changes in land use and farming methods. Fortunately they recolonised and made a natural comeback to Cornwall in 2001 when three were spotted on the Lizard Peninsula. With help and protection wild chough numbers are slowly but steadily increasing and in 1987 Operation Chough was established by Paradise Park Wildlife Sanctuary at Hayle, with the specific aim of seeing the chough thriving again in Cornwall. As an indication of just how rare they are, the total number in Cornwall in 2014 was estimated to be fewer than 40.

SEAGULLS

The Cornish for seagull is *goolan*. They are widespread in Cornwall and multitudes can be seen daily. They are aggressive, scavenging opportunists, nature's vacuum cleaners, always ready for a meal be it natural or courtesy of us humans. Juveniles use their beaks to tap on the red spot on their parents' beak when they want to be fed. Ignore the signs that say 'DO NOT FEED THE SEAGULLS' at your peril. Gulls are rather partial to pasties or tasty fish and chips, so beware! Just like babies, gulls seem to cry out all the time and are rather cunning creatures. They can drink seawater as they have glands over their eyes that excrete the salt, which can sometimes be seen dripping from their nose and beak. Another clever trick is they drop shellfish from a height onto hard ground or rocks to crack them open. When they want a worm they sometimes dance on soil or sand and the vibrations bring the worms to the surface. Gulls are intelligent, never missing a trick and as some can live for over 30 years; that's a lot of time to perfect their skills. In recent years experiments with seagull control using birds of prey as a deterrent have been highly successful and there is now a call for this to be fully introduced.

CORNISH REX

The Cornish for cat is *cath* and Cornwall has an amazing species, namely the Cornish Rex. In 1950 a litter of five kittens were born on a farm in the Bodmin Moor area. Four of the kittens were normal in appearance but one, named Kallibunker, was very different indeed. He had unusually larger ears, curly whiskers and a short curly coat of fur that could be very much likened to waves of crushed velvet, making him look rather like a cat with a tight perm. They are incredibly distinctive cats with their sleek appearance, being likened to a feline greyhound, yet many people have never even seen one. Sadly Kallibunker died in 1956 but his hugely popular descendants still thrive and his name is internationally revered within cat breeding circles.

CORNISH ELM

In Cornish tree is *gwedhen*. The iconic Cornish elm was once common throughout the whole of Cornwall until Dutch elm disease took its terrible toll. The good news is that because of strong new sucker growth from live tree roots, combined with natural hybridisation and the fungal mutation of the disease itself, the future may not be entirely over for the Cornish elm just yet, so fingers crossed for *Ulmus stricta*.

PISKIES

Cornish piskie charms are traditionally meant to bring their owner good luck. They are sold in great numbers, generally as novelty holiday mementos. Usually they are depicted as little men with pointed ears, red hair, green clothing and, unlike their fairy (or faerie) cousins, with no wings. They are allegedly fun-loving little fellows and relish playing in water, dancing in moonlight and tricking others with their practical jokes. Piskies (or pixies) often create illusions and try to confuse travellers in the hope of making them totally and utterly lost, although wearing a coat inside out apparently stops this from happening. Some old Cornish homes have holes specially built into their walls to let piskies in, as they sometimes bestow good deeds. One type of piskie known as Jack o' Lanterns apparently even showed favoured miners where rich mineral deposits were located.

EMMETS

The emmet is a very common mammal in Cornwall. The name is derived from St Emmet himself, the revered brother of St Piran, who was alleged to have first introduced the species into North Cornwall. Although found throughout the Duchy they are rarely listed in wildlife books. They are abundant in the summer months but less so during the winter. The emmet population thrives here in vast colonies and in just one season millions can briefly visit Cornwall. This highly social mammal is a biped, often seen sporting lurid plumage and feeding mostly in daylight hours and early evenings. The young of the species may cause problems, as can the adolescent strutting males once they have flown the nest. Mating at this time is a priority. The parents often turn a blind eye when out with the fledglings and can themselves be problematic. Cornish folk love emmets when they flock to the Duchy in great numbers during the season but many are likewise happy to see them return home again. In reality 'emmet' is actually a rather jovial word the Cornish use to describe tourists, likening them to ants rushing round everywhere! It's from the Cornish dialect word *aemete* ironically derived from Old English, which eventually converted into the modern word ant. In Cornish the actual word for ant is *moryon*.

A Taste of Cornwall

Cornwall's food heritage is so much more than just cream teas, clotted cream fudge and Cornish pasties. Quality fresh food from land and sea is thankfully a very familiar item nowadays and high-class cuisine is nearly as common as take-away fish and chips. Locally sourced produce is always worth seeking out as it is not only exceptionally tasty but also great for the Cornish economy. Sadly some of the more traditional Cornish foods are not as popular as they once were, so included in this section are a few that are well worth saving and certainly worth sampling. Muggety Pie sounds interesting but be warned it's main ingredient is offal and Cornish Raw Fry sounds uncooked but actually is, being a combination of frying and boiling. Dippy sounds silly but is actually rather tasty, being sardines and potato boiled in single cream! Traditional Cornish Under-Roast is simply a delicious one-pot meat dish with the meat (usually beef) being slow cooked on a bed of potatoes. Rock or Jubilee Cornish game on a menu are simply Cornish breeds of hen in the form of young chickens and not true game birds like pheasant or partridge. Before the days of cast iron cooking ranges many a Cornish home used a clome (or cloam, meaning clay) oven, somewhat similar to modern day pizza ovens but without a chimney, being built into the side of a fireplace chimney-breast and with a removable door. Many still exist, some having been bricked up for centuries and there is a lovely exposed example in Tintagel Old Post Office, a former 14th century manor house.

CORNISH PASTIES

The Cornish for this delicacy is *pasti*, with pasties being *pastiow*, or in Old Cornish *hoggan/hogen*, which originally referred to its pork meat filling. Incidentally 'pasty' actually means made of paste, of strong dough and when filled with seasoned meat and vegetables to create a 'turnover pie' and cooked to perfection it creates a dish-less, hand held, all in one, mobile meal. The pastry casing has to be strong so that it doesn't collapse when held. A pie in Cornish is a pasty and, rather obviously, Cornish pasties are just referred to as pasties in Cornwall. They are commonly known as oggies with over five million annually consumed in Cornwall alone and over 120 million produced there every year. The word *croust* (from crust) is a Cornish term meaning pasty time, when miners took a food break from their work and is sometimes still used to mean a bite to eat. The ancient Phoenicians (1200-539 BC) came to Cornwall to trade tin and it's said that the shape of a pasty can be likened to a quarter moon with rounded ends, which represents the emblem of their goddess Astarte. The earliest reference to pasties in literature is from the French poet Chretien de Troyes who in c1170 wrote the lengthy Arthurian poem 'Erec (Eric) & Enide'. Pasties are mentioned by the character Guivret and in the tale both she and Erec are from Cornwall.

Pasties are now a worldwide gastronomic delicacy, despite having their origins in the unglamorous Cornish mining industry. Being stuck underground on a long shift, Cornish miners needed a substantial midday meal and hence the pasty was born. Its traditional, thick, crimped edge was a holding handle, being thrown away afterwards by the dirty-handed miner. The filling (cooked from raw) was a matter of taste but usually involved steak, onion or leek, swede/yellow turnip and potato, in varying proportions depending on where in Cornwall it was made. The Cornish call a swede a turnip, referring to the confusing Swedish ('Swede') yellow turnip. The use of carrot is considered sacrilegious. Rump steak gives rich, tasty gravy within a pasty and for many people diced meat is certainly far preferable to mincing it. Strangely enough fish is not a common ingredient anymore. In days long gone pasties were often made with such meats as veal, mutton, pigeon, conger eel and pilchard. Often one corner of the pasty contained some sort of sweet, fruit filling. Frequently the owner had his name, initials or symbol baked into the pastry for ease of identification. Some miners would often leave a small piece of pasty to appease the spirits ('knockers') of the mine. Not doing so might result in their displeasure, leading to such bad luck as falling stones, barren seams or worse. Sadly the mines are all but a relic of the past now but the pasty lives on forever. There are many Cornish fishermen who won't have pasties onboard their boats as they consider it unlucky.

Cornish pasties were granted Protected Geographical Indication (PGI) status in 2011, meaning if they are not made in Cornwall or stray from a strict set of prescribed rules then they cannot legally be called 'Cornish' pasties. Following this the first World Pasty Championships (Oggie Olympics) were held just before St Piran's Day in March 2012 at the Eden Project and are now a prodigious annual event concluding with a grand 'Oggy Oscars' party. Morvah celebrates a Pasty Day every August and Redruth holds an annual three-day extravaganza Cornish Pasty Festival. Another contentious issue reguarding pasties in general is the actual positioning of the crimping, as some have it to the side whilst others locate it at the top. The PGI ruling controversially favours only side crimping, thus instantly rendering many genuine top crimped Cornish pasties 'illegal' - doubly so as their shape doesn't comply with the prescribed 'D' shape ruling either, although whichever way they are made they still taste superb.

There is also much debate concerning other pasty related topics such as shape, left or right handed crimping techniques, traditional filling versus modern alternatives, the vegetarian/vegan option, potato variety, sliced or diced potato, the great carrot controversy, beef skirt versus chuck and flank, mass production, the swede/turnip debate, flour strength, pastry texture and type, glazing, 'gravy' leakage, seasoning, savoury cornered 'two course' pasties, best eaten hot or cold and other such vital matters. Food for thought indeed and that's without discussing the highly contentious ongoing pasty dispute with neighbouring Devon!

Pasties are produced by a wide variety of makers, some being large commercial concerns and others much smaller and more local. Many people consider pasties bought where they are locally made and then wrapped in paper are far superior to the more commercially produced ones sold in plastic wrappers and exported outside Cornwall, so why not put their theory to the test? Have fun sampling as many as possible before deciding on a favourite! The choice is endless. Take into account such things as appearance, flavour, meat content, general filling, pastry texture and cost. Happy *pasti* hunting!

HOG'S PUDDING

This pork delicacy is rather similar to black pudding but very pale in colour due its total lack of blood as an ingredient. It's sometimes referred to as white pudding (or, rarely, as Cornish haggis) although it's not served as a pudding after a main meal at all but usually fried as part of a full Cornish breakfast (which is similar to a full English breakfast but much tastier!). Often it's made in the form of a large, spiced sausage and is a tasty compliment to the morning feast. It's well worth trying and is far nicer than its name suggests!

CAUDLE CHICKEN PIE

This delicious chicken pie also contains onions, milk and parsley. When almost cooked, a thick 'caudle' (warm) mixture of beaten egg and cream is poured into the pie through a hole in the crust. The whole thing is then left to set and eaten cold. This dish would be a rare find indeed on a modern day menu but it's worth enquiring about just in case, especially in a delicatessen. Cornish Charter Pie is another type of rich and creamy chicken dish most likely having its origins in medieval times as celebratory food for a Charter Fair or Charter Market.

CREAM TEAS

What an iconic concept a cream tea actually is, being a combination of fresh scones, jam and clotted cream (butter is optional) all washed down with a pot of steaming hot tea. Traditionally the scone can be substituted for a Cornish split, which is a bread roll with a little sugar added to the mix. It's less heavy than a scone and contains no raisins. Another possibility is when treacle is substituted for the jam, which is charmingly referred to as Thunder & Lightening due to the black and yellow colour of the filling and it goes down a storm! Variations on this involve golden syrup or honey. The term clotted is derived from the Cornish word *clout* meaning thick like leather, which describes the cream perfectly. The Cornish for cream is *dehen* and it's believed that when the ancient Phoenicians were trading for tin they shared with the Cornish their ancient recipe for kaymak, a product similar to clotted cream. Rodda's clotted cream with its origins in Redruth since 1890 seems to be the most abundant commercial brand sold in the Duchy, although there are many other excellent commercial and home made varieties available. In 1924 Fanny Rodda cleverly perfected longer lasting cream, which revolutionised the industry. In 1998 the European Union (EU) gave the accolade of Protected Designation of Origin (PDO) status to Cornish Clotted Cream, which in order to qualify as authentic has to be manufactured in Cornwall using milk with a fat content of 55% or more obtained from Cornish cows and made in a traditional way that results in golden crust formation. The end result is a sheer, rich, blissful delight.

The very best Cornish cream teas are of course all locally sourced; apart from the tea-leaves you might obviously think, but in fact there's even a Cornish tea plantation at Tregothnan near Truro! Camellias grow well in Cornwall and tea is obtained from a special species of the plant, namely *Camellia sinensis*. Only the tender young growing tips are harvested, usually from April to October and all by hand. The young leaves are quickly processed and packaged to become genuine Cornish tea-leaves, all ready to use. Tregothnan even exports some of its tea crop to China and India. The Cornish for tea is *te*, milk is *leth* and sugar is *shogra*. A dilemma that needs careful thought and a great deal of practical experimentation is what actually goes onto the scone/Cornish split first, the jam or the clotted cream? Jam on first is the Cornish way and jam on last is the Devon way: 'Jam then cream is the Cornish dream but its cream then jam for the Devon man'. The Cornish say they are far too proud of their clotted cream to hide it beneath a load of jam and a scientific study concludes that the Devon method risks the jam slipping off the cream, so best to side with the experts and do it the Cornish way!

CORNISH COFFEE

The Cornish for coffee is *koffi*. Cornish coffee beans were first harvested in the humid tropics biome of the Eden Project (see 75) in 2007 and were on limited sale as actual coffee at Jamie Oliver's Fifteen Cornwall restaurant at Watergate Bay, Newquay, in January 2008. The crop only made about 50 very rare cups of coffee in total. The chance came about when bar manager Tristan Stevenson of the Fifteen restaurant noticed coffee beans growing at the Eden Project as part of the exhibits. He realised an opportunity and the resulting coffee became the first ever to be made from beans grown in the UK. More harvesting may be considered and if so then perhaps Cornish coffee production could flourish. As a start the Eden Project would be ideal, with profits aiding their valuable research and conservation work.

SAFFRON CAKE

Cake is *tesen* in Cornish and a slice or two of saffron cake is like golden Cornish sunshine glowing on a plate. The word saffron literally means yellow and it may be that whilst trading in Cornwall for tin the ancient Phoenicians first introduced it to the Cornish. In truth saffron cake is really a loaf as it's made with yeast bread but whatever the name, saffron is definitely the key ingredient. For subtle flavour and delicate colour authentic saffron must always be used in preference to the cheaper, inferior, saffron essence or yellow dye. It takes something like four thousand flowers from the crocus sativus plant to produce a mere 30g of saffron, which consists of only the dried female stigma part of the flower. Being hand picked it's no wonder that saffron commands high prices, which is why it's treated with the utmost respect and only used very sparingly. Saffron cake was traditionally eaten on Good Friday and at Christmas but is now enjoyed all year round, as are saffron rolls, which are sometimes referred to as revel buns, originally for a very special occasion. Both are commonly available and purchased freshly baked are simply delicious. Some say saffron cake should only be eaten indoors but it's a tradition that's extremely hard to keep!

STAR GAZY PIE

Every year in Mousehole (see 60) on the night before Christmas Eve, Star Gazy fish pies are consumed in memory of the sixteenth century fisherman Tom Bawcock and his heroic deed when he saved the village from starvation. The legend goes that whilst other locals stayed within the safety of the harbour, Tom braved the storms of winter and went out to catch some fish for everyone. Despite the dangers he returned safely to Mousehole with a boatload of seven sorts of fish to share and so all the villagers were saved. A fish pie was then duly baked with the fish heads exposed just to prove they had indeed been caught and cooked. The event is known as Tom Bawcock's Eve and is an incredibly popular event. Nowadays the harbour is protected in the winter months by a sturdy barrier across the harbour entrance so that the fury of the sea is kept at bay. The village goes overboard with its Christmas lights and decorations, with the Ship Inn at the centre of festivities. In Cornish the word for star is *steren*.

FAIRING BISCUITS

These lightly spiced, flat, sweet biscuits were originally sold at feasts, fairs and markets. In Cornish biscuit is *tesen gales*. Fairing literally means a fair gift and these biscuits were part of that gift together with fruit and sweets. They could be plain or iced, even gilded with genuine gold leaf and were often sold in various interesting and appealing shapes such as animals and humans, hence the origins of ginger bread men. The fairing biscuit may well have started at the Launceston hiring fairs where farmers took on temporary workers to help with crop gathering. It's the flavour of ginger, cinnamon and mixed spice that sets these biscuits apart from the rest. In 1886

Cornish baker John Cooper Furniss started a highly successful fairing biscuit business, which is still in production today. Fairings have now evolved into having a large variety of flavours such as saffron, vanilla and almond.

HEVVA CAKE

While the men folk of a fishing village were busy heaving in pilchard nets the women would bake a hevva cake, now known as heavy cake. It's actually not really a cake at all but more a rich pastry slice laden with currents and is traditionally marked on the top with a criss-cross net pattern in celebration of the catch in the fishing mesh. *Hevva* is a Cornish word for a shoal of fish and the Cornish word for cake is *tesen.*

FIGGIE HOBBIN

This dish is also referred to as Figgie 'Obbin and is the Cornish equivalent of a plum duff pudding. Strangely enough there are no figs inside the suet pastry but raisins, as the Cornish refer to them as figs. It could be that this figgie dessert was kept warm on the hob of the old wood or coal fire, hence the derivation of part of the name. Cornish Fuggan is similar but without the suet.

WHORTLEBERRY PIE

Whortleberry is simply the Cornish name for the bilberry (*Vaccinium uliginosum*), which is rather similar to the blueberry both in colour and taste but is smaller and the berries grow in little groups rather than large clusters. They can be harvested on moor and heathland in late summer and early autumn. These soft, delicate berries make a wonderful free ingredient in this traditional Cornish fruit pie. The berries can be made into jam for use with a cream tea and it's believed that they aid vision. Whortleberries are cram-packed full of goodness and are as beneficial as the highly rated cranberry.

GILLYFLOWER PIE

This wonderfully sounding dish is simply a special type of apple pie using the rare Cornish gilliflower apple (*Malus domestica*), a late seasoned, medium large, old dessert variety. It has a knobbly, roundish, conical shape, is purplish-red and was first found growing in a Truro cottage garden in 1800. Its firm, juicy flesh has an unusual sweet, rich, clove or melon-like fragrance and taste. Cooks sometimes add cloves to apple pies but this wondrous fruit already had a built in supply. Old-fashioned clove scented pinks (dianthus) were nicknamed gilliflowers and were sometimes used in cooking as a cheap clove substitute.

KELLY'S ICE CREAM

The Cornish for ice cream is *dehen rew* and for over a century Kelly's, the oldest and leading ice cream manufacturers in the Duchy, has been making the genuine article. Their delicious product uses only Cornish clotted cream and fresh milk from Cornish herds and has scooped many awards over the years. The Italian Staffieri family originally came over here in the late 1800s and established their 'iced cream' business, first in St Austell then finally in Bodmin and the result is frozen perfection, partly distributed by a distinctive fleet of vans. Cornish clotted cream is not just reserved for such delights as cream teas, cakes and fudge, as it's also delicious combined with ice cream!

CORNISH BEER & CIDER

Brewing both beer and cider is a cottage industry that's been going on for countless years and the end result is wonderful. Old Cornish beer and cider houses were a very popular alternative to the inns of the day, especially with miners, fishermen and smugglers. They were fondly known as kiddlywinks (or kiddleywinks) and no doubt also had smuggled wines and spirits on offer to tickle the taste buds of their thirsty clientele. There is a famously strong and enormously popular beer known as White Ale that was brewed throughout Cornwall in the Middle Ages. It was apparently so thick (due to egg white) that it resembled buttered ale and production finished around 1877. When Cornish miners emigrated to seek their fortunes abroad, especially to Australia, these Cousin Jacks as they were nicknamed were famed for making a sophisticated brew for special occasions and festivities. It was known as Swanky Beer, which is still at the hub of the celebrations in a handful of old Australian copper mining towns that celebrate the Kernowek Lowender festival.

Nowadays there are many pubs serving excellent real ales and wonderful food, the tastiest being locally sourced. Cornwall has a wealth of fine breweries making superb liquid refreshment and some are award-winning companies. The Cornish for beer is *korev* and *pinta korev marpleg* translates as 'a pint of beer please'. Beer garden is *lowarth korev* and cheers is *sewena*. Cornish beers perfectly compliment local meals of freshly caught produce such as fish, crab, lobster etc and of course the almost obligatory Cornish pasty. The Wetherspoon's chain of pubs has signage in both English and Cornish in order to promote the use and development of the Cornish language and individual premises have thus been included in this book. The pubs all hold regular Cornish ale festivals and proudly celebrate St Piran's Day every 5th March. There is some superb Cornish cider and scrumpy to choose from but beware as it's often rather strong! Pear cider/perry is a refreshing alternative to apple cider but again, take care as it can be just as potent! If in doubt perhaps opt instead for some sparkling and wonderful Cornish 'champagne'!

CORNISH WINE

Setting, soil and climate single out Cornwall as being an excellent location for quality wine production. In Cornish wine is *gwin*. There are many delightful Cornish wines such as those from the vineyards of the Camel Valley, Barras Moor, Bosue, Lambourne, Pemboa, Polgoon and Polmassick. Visitors to the vineyards are usually most welcome and wine tasting is an added bonus. A traditional Cornish drink is shrub, which is basically an alcoholic herb wine cordial traditionally mixed with dark rum or perhaps brandy.

Cornish Mead is a honey-based sweet wine, often referred to as the honeymoon drink and is simply enchanting. Another mead type drink is metheglin, which is based on fermented honey with added herbs or spices.

CORNISH SPIRIT

In 2011 the first batch of genuine Cornish Whiskey was produced by a partnership between the St Austell Brewery and Healey's Cyder Farm. It was first fermented in 2003 in the smallest legal still in the country and matured for seven years, after which the Hicks and Healey Cornish Single Malt Whiskey was officially born and was the first to be produced in Cornwall for over 300 years. Healey's Cyder Farm at Callestick, near Perranporth, has also produced a Cornish Apple Cyder Brandy, the first again to be made in Cornwall for over 300 years. Distilling started in 2000 as part of a millennium project. Healey's Cyder Farm is a great place to visit and guided tours can even be taken round their distillery. Elemental Cornish Gin is lovingly hand crafted by the Cornish Gin Distillery (est 2013) within the Duchy at Tregonetha, St Columb Major, near Newquay. Another manufacturer of Cornish gin is the Southwestern Distillery (est 2012) at St Ervan, Wadebridge, near Padstow, producing delicious Tarquin's Gin. Look out for Mahogany, a Cornish sailor's and fisherman's tipple consisting of two parts gin to one part black treacle! Aval Dor is an amazing, deliciously sweet and creamy premium Cornish vodka, distilled at Colwith Farm, Treesmill, Par, St Austell. The unusual name comes from the Cornish for potato as the vodka is derived from the King Edward variety.

CORNISH CHEESE

Cows and goats feeding on the lush grass of Cornwall produce wonderfully rich, creamy milk, which in turn makes excellent cheese. In Cornish cheese is *keus* and this is just a small selection; many award winning, showcasing what's available from the vast and varied Cornish cheese board. Cornish Yarg is a wonderfully creamy, semi-firm, moist cheese, having a slight mushroom-musty tang and uniquely has an edible, hand applied nettle-leaf (no sting) rind, which is an art form in its own right. Yarg is simply Gray backwards, which is the surname of the farmer in whose attic the old recipe, said to have its origins in the 13th century, was found. Also available is Wild Garlic Yarg, which has a rind made from naturally grown wild garlic leaves. Cornish Blue is beautifully soft, mild, creamy sweet and is a mellower version of the usual sort of blue varieties. It's eaten as a young cheese and a must to experience. Olde Smokey is a mellow, semi-firm, sweet flavoured, smooth and creamy handmade cheese. It lives up to its name by having a heady, smoke aroma and a superb taste derived from it being smoked over fragrant Cornish fruit tree chippings. Its golden yellowy-orange colour just speaks volumes about its flavour. Gevrik is a white, full fat, soft goat's milk cheese, having a creamy, nutty flavour. The name means small goat in Cornish. Cornish Brie is a soft, mild, very creamy and delicious cheese. Because it's made using rich Cornish milk, beneath its white rind it's a delicate yellow buttery colour. Keltic Gold is a soft, creamy, pungent organic cheese having an edible, tasty rind that's been dipped in cider. Cornish Crumbly is a zingy, sharp, fresh tasting, semi-hard cheese.

North Cornwall

The rugged coast of North Cornwall stretches from Marsland Valley Nature Reserve near Bude right down to Land's End. This is roughly a distance of about 140 miles or so and the Cornwall Coastal Path follows it round as it hugs the Celtic Sea area of the Atlantic Ocean. The sea with all its untamed beauty is a joy to behold and the whole area is a precious Cornish gem well worth exploring.

BUDE

In Cornish Bude is known as Porthbud and is Cornwall's most northerly town. The Cornish coastal boundary with Devon is but a few miles away in the Marsland Valley Nature Reserve at Marsland Water. Bude has also been known as Budeham, Bude Haven, and even Bede Haven, meaning harbour of the holy men. The name could well be a corruption of Bede, the venerable Benedictine monk. Some claim Bude to be the birthplace of British surfing (surf riding) rather than Newquay and its beaches are often described by Australians as the Bondi of Britain. The sport was established here sometime in the 1940s and the Bude Surf Life Saving Club followed in 1953, inspired by Australians spreading the surfing word far and wide. Years ago the eccentric Reverend Robert Stephen Hawker (1803-1875) sometimes hung around Bude's beautiful Summerleaze and Crooklets beaches dressed up as a mermaid in order to serenade passers by. He wanted them to believe there really were mermaids and that they were alive and well and living at Bude! In 1825 he wrote *Song of the Western Men*, which is used as the unofficial Cornish National Anthem of unity (see 9) and in 1843 he introduced the first ever Harvest Festival service at his church in nearby Morwenstow. The open air and tidally fed Bude Sea Pool Lido (1930) provides great fun and is located at Summerleaze Beach. Look out for small, rare, Carboniferous fossil fish, which are occasionally exposed in the local coastal rock deposits.

Sir Goldsworthy Gurney, a brilliant Cornish inventor, built a local house by the Wharf in 1830 named the Castle or Bude Castle.

It was deliberately built on moving sand just to prove it could be done! It's still standing so his master plan actually worked. His fascinating home is now open to the public and is known as the Bude Castle Heritage Centre. It was originally lit with his Bude Light system, which ran by cleverly combining oxygen, oil lamps, prisms and mirrors. Using this bright idea he also lit up the Houses of Parliament, Trafalgar Square, various theatres and numerous lighthouses. His light system was patented in 1839 and so was a Gurney Stove heating system in 1856. Gurney was one of the leading pioneers in designing and building steam-powered road carriages and in 1829 one such 'car' reached the amazing speed of around 14 miles per hour! Queen Victoria knighted him in 1863 but sadly Sir Goldsworthy Gurney died penniless in 1875 and was buried at the nearby Launcells parish church of St Swithin's. In the millennium year of 2000 a tall, thin, colourful cone was erected in honour of the Bude Light system and is located close to his Castle home near the bandstand. Known as the Bude Light 2000, it resembles a giant example of a container you can buy on holiday filled with different coloured stripes of sand. It was created by sculptor Carole Vincent and is actually made of concrete, with the colours representing sky, sand and sea. It contains fibre-optic lights that look simply stunning at night.

The local landmark Nanny Moore's Bridge at Granville Terrace was apparently named after a beach attendant (a dipper) who once lived nearby. The Cornish Way, a 180-mile bicycle route stretching mostly inland from Bude to Land's End was established in 2000, part of the popular National Cycle Network. Bude canal was first opened in the 1820s but sadly competition from the railway forced its closure in 1891. In its hay-day the inclined plane system of raising vessels to higher levels was in use here rather than just having more locks. It's rather a rare canal as it has a set of lock gates that open directly out to sea. In the past fierce storms have ripped these clean off, demonstrating the immense strength of the sea, a force never to be underestimated. The canal once extended 35 miles all the way to

Launceston and was used to carry seaweed and lime-rich shell sand to improve the farmland soils further inland, as well as transporting a variety of other goods. Luckily a few miles of it are still open for all to enjoy. It's purely recreational now and abundant with wildlife, including sightings of otters. Bude canal is a fisherman's dream and close by the River Neet flows into the sea. Near the sea-lock end of the canal is the Bude-Stratton Museum; the entrance fee is nominal and the museum is housed in what was the old canal company's smithy.

Guarding the headland above the canal on part of the Coastal Path stands Compass Point Tower, which draws curious visitors like a ship to a wrecker's light. It was originally named the Tower of the Winds, although some refer to it as the Pepper Pot. It looks like an old place of worship but was actually a coastguard shelter built for Sir Thomas Acland in the 1820s. Octagonal in shape, the eight points of the compass are carved in capitals each of its sides, high up by the roof. It was moved to this position in the 1880s when cliff erosion threatened to locate it rapidly downhill from its original spot. Nearby is the glorious Widemouth Bay, which is well worth walking to along the Cornish Coastal Path. A little further on is Millook beach, which is a surfer's paradise and given the right conditions is apparently one of the finest left-hand reef breaks in the whole of Europe. The rock strata in the cliffs here are highly folded and this geological crumple zone 'Geosite' is famous worldwide. On a clear day from Bude there is a spectacular view over the bay to a cluster of satellite dishes sited on the old RAF WWII airfield at Cleave, near Coombe, Morwenstow. It's the top secret Government Communications Headquarters composite signals intelligence base, known as GCHQ Bude, a government command centre. In fact it's so top secret that it's not even marked on maps for security reasons, which is rather strange really as it's a huge complex visible from miles away. Devon's unspoilt, granite island of Lundy can also be seen about 20 miles out to sea and seems to suddenly materialise like a ghostly spectre on the distant horizon. Its isolation appears to be both its strength and appeal. It's a wildlife haven although accommodation for visitors there is strictly limited. Some believe it to be the ancient Arthurian Isle of Avalon.

BOSCASTLE

Boscastle has a Norman castle, of the Motte and Bailey type, or at least the remains of one. Bottreux Castle is situated above the harbour and was said to be in ruins by 1478. It's now little more than just a mound of earth. The French Bottreaux (or Botterrel) family built it and hence the name Boscastle came into being as a corruption of Bottreaux, in Cornish Kastel Boterel. Boscastle lies in the bottom of a valley surrounded by steep hills, like some sort of huge sausage-shaped amphitheatre at the base of a Norwegian fjord. Boscastle has been described by many as the village that survived and it certainly has, with a seemingly endless supply of grace and style.

Terrible floods hit Boscastle on the 16th August 2004 causing an estimated 50 million pounds worth of damage. A twelve-foot high river of floodwater and mud devastated the luckless village. Many buildings were washed away or badly damaged and the television images that flashed around the world showing the disaster actually unfolding were unforgettable. Cars floated away towards the harbour, with a total of 84 actually found in it afterwards, as helicopter crew's plucked people to safety and even one lucky Alsatian named Izzy. Miraculously nobody died although in 1958 a flood here did result in a fatality. After 2004 the Environmental Agency spent over ten million pounds on structural repairs just widening and deepening the river channel, giving it increased capacity and so making it safer in flood situations. Strangely, the village nowadays seems little altered. The rebuild is a tribute to all who had a hand in it. Boscastle has risen out of its tragedy like a phoenix from the ashes and is a true marvel of rebirth.

The outside of the Wellington Hotel looks just like a superior golf clubhouse. It's nicknamed the Welly and used to be called the Bos Castle Hotel. It was renamed after the death of the 1st Duke Of

Wellington who died in 1852. Several ghosts allegedly haunt this 16th century inn. Further up the hill is a rival pub ironically named the Napoleon. The Long Bar of the Welly has four splendid old glass panels depicting the four quarters of the Royal Standard. They were specially commissioned to celebrate Queen Victoria's only visit to Cornwall in 1848. There are also three small, fine, brass lamps with red glass bases hanging from the ceiling by the bar, which were donated by the author Thomas Hardy in 1872. The once ancient 300 year old Harbour Light tearoom (formally Pixie House) was washed away in the flood leaving just a heap of rubble but the building has been completely rebuilt, even down to the wobble in its twisty roof. The replacement stands as a testament to the skill and craftsmanship of others and to man's determination in the face of disaster. An old coffee jar time capsule once hidden there was eventually found after the flood, having been washed up on a Devon beach and later returned. The Boscastle Camelot Pottery (est 1967) is well worth visiting for its delicate dendritic Mochaware products.

A visit to the quaint Witchcraft Museum (est 1960) and the old Cobweb Inn is a must and inside the National Trust Tourist Centre are several wonderful local history displays including ones on the flood itself. Thomas Hardy (1840-1928) met his first wife Emma Gifford in Boscastle village and wrote the novel *A Pair Of Blue Eyes* for her in 1899, in which Boscastle is referred to as Castle Boterel. Both he and John Betjamin wrote in and around the area and it certainly is an inspirational place. At the harbour entrance can be found the Boscastle Blowhole, also known as the Devil's Bellows and at high tide a fountain of sea water can sometimes been seen spurting out of it; often the wind can be heard moaning and howling through it. During the war years a stray mine blew up the outer harbour arm in 1941, which could have led to a far more serious incident than in fact it did. There is a legend concerning the lost bells of Boscastle: it's said that the silent tower of nearby Forrabury church has no bells because they were lost in the bay during the time of the plague when the ship carrying them was wrecked. Apparently the eerie tolling bells can sometimes be heard on the winds of local storms and by divers in the area. At nearby Trethevy is located the St Necten's (or St Nectan's) Glen, an ancient, pre-Christian site where strips of cloth known as clouties are ritually tied to nearby trees. Strangely enough it was named not after a saint at all but after the ancient water god Nechtan.

TINTAGEL

This village should really be called Trevena, as Tintagel is actually only the name of the headland. In Cornish Tintagel is called Tre war Venydh and in old Cornish was named Dundagil, meaning the impregnable castle. Tintagel is obsessed by Arthurian legend and his name and everything associated with it pop up all over the place. In Fore Street can be found the much photographed Old Post Office, a 14th century farmhouse and a National Trust property since 1903. King Arthur's Great Halls (1860) are also located in Fore Street. They are huge and were further extended for benevolent millionaire Frederick T. Glasscock who made his money from, of all things… custard. From 1927 through to 1936 he used the building for his wonderfully named 'Order of the Fellowship of the Knights of the Round Table'. The building is open to the public and contains 72 magnificent Pre-Raphaelite stained-glass windows depicting King Arthur's story, designed by a pupil of William Morris. The Cornishman Inn is well worth a visit if just to escape some of the more blatant commercialism of the village.

Worldwide Tintagel is known and described as King Arthur country and that it certainly thrives on, but was he actually born here? Did he ever live here? The legend is certainly very strong but the facts are rather hazy. Tintagel's mystical castle together with its Arthurian associations is definitely Tintagel's main attraction and international claim to fame. This atmospheric ruin, first opened to the public in 1852, holds a panoramic viewpoint and was the supposed stronghold of Arthur, King of Britain. The medieval fortress was built in 1233, sadly hundreds of years after King Arthur's death, which is a huge blow for both tourism and the legend itself. However it's not all doom and gloom, as earlier 5th to 6th century Dark Age remains of a royal citadel do exist here, together with evidence of extensive foreign trading, so the tale could have a basis of truth to it after all. Arthur was the first-born son and thus heir to the throne of King Uther Pendragon, King of England. When Uther died Merlin the magician raised baby Arthur in secret and later came all the adventures with the sword etc. When King Arthur eventually died he apparently ended up in Avalon but was Arthur in reality a Celtic chief of the late fifth or early sixth century who was fighting against the Anglo-Saxons? Cornwall certainly lays claim to Arthur and his fame and to back this up pottery has unquestionably been found here of the right era for King Arthur. Perhaps Camelot is in the vicinity as Camelford and the River Camel are! In 1998 a slate inscription was unearthed on the castle site bearing the Latin wording *Pater Coliavificit Artognov*, meaning 'Artognou, father of a descendant of Coll, had this built'. Artognou is pronounced 'Arth-nou' and certainly sounds rather like Arthur. For now the jury seems to be out but the plot thickens.

The rather isolated twelfth century church of St Materiana is located on the cliff top close to the coastal path and is well worth visiting, if only for the stained-glass windows, the fascinating graveyard and the awe-inspiring views. Blackways Cove near Trebarwith Strand is where many a shipwreck has occurred over the years. The cove is allegedly haunted and one such local ghost is said to be that of a vindictive son whose father died leaving his farm to the other brother. The youngest got nothing and in a jealous rage burnt down the farm, only to find that his kind and generous brother had died the previous day and left it all to him in his will. That simple twist of fate weighed heavily on his conscience and as a ghost he supposedly still wanders the area racked with guilt, having effectively burned down his own farm. The story is known as the legend of Blackways Cove and the ruins of the farm are still to be found.

LAUNCESTON

Launceston has been referred to as the gateway to Cornwall and in Cornish is known as Lannstevan, meaning church of St Stephen. The old market town stronghold of Launceston was once the ancient capital of Cornwall and was known as Dunheved in Saxon times, meaning the swelling hill. Its appearance is magnificent, complete with a superb ruined Norman castle and the impressive St Mary Magdalene church with its ornate 16th century carved granite exterior. On the castle green gruesome public executions used to occur. The packhorse Prior's Bridge, the medieval gateway of South Gate Arch (this was the only walled town in Cornwall) and the narrow-gauge Launceston Steam Railway in St Thomas Road are all a must for visitors, as is the castle and St Mary Magdalene church. The Lawrence House Museum in Castle Street has free entry (donations welcome) and is housed in an attractive Georgian house constructed in 1753. The Launceston Steam Railway (summer only) runs for two and a half miles to New Mills and nearby is the Tamar Otter and Wildlife Centre at North Petherwin. The Penpont Brewery (est 2008) is located at Altarnun.

CAMELFORD

In Cornish Camelford is Reskammel and translated means Kammelford. It was once known as Cam Pol meaning the winding river, namely the River Camel and the town grew around its ford. Camelford was a medieval market town and is now a tourist haven, although somewhat spoilt by the A39 road. The Town Hall has a weather vane in the shape of a camel and although the creatures are not indigenous there are live camels in Cornwall! Yes there really are, sadly not here in Camelford but near Helston (see 65). The North Cornwall Museum and Gallery at The Clease was opened in 1974. The nearby Camel Trail for cyclists and walkers is highly recommended and follows the route of the river. The world famous Delabole Slate Quarry is close by and tours of the site are well worth taking. Slaughterbridge is said to be the site of a great battle between King Arthur and his nephew Mordred. The Arthurian Centre here certainly supports the notion and displays an ancient inscribed stone reputed to be King Arthur's tombstone, circa AD 540. In 1848 the poet Alfred (Lord) Tennyson believed it to be so. Not far away is the village of St Tudy where in 1754 William Bligh was born and later achieved notoriety as Captain Bligh, being the main cause of the 1789 mutiny on HMS *Bounty*.

PORT ISAAC

Port Isaac is a typical picturesque Cornish-fishing village with lobster pots piled upon the jetty and quaint whitewashed cottages clinging to the sides of the valley. Everything is close together and cosy. It has been described as just what the doctor ordered; a place to relax, unwind and to just listen to the sea. In Cornish it's known as Porthysek, which means corn port. The old Cornish word for corn is *yzack*. Slate was once an export here but now *Doc Martin* and the Fishermen's Friends chart topping male choir are. The very mention of Port Isaac means one thing to many television viewers and that's the programme *Doc Martin*. The series starring Martin Clunes of *Men Behaving Badly* fame was filmed here, with Port Isaac being renamed Port Wenn (Portwenn), which is a clever play on the Cornish place name for nearby Port Quin, namely Porth Gwynn. As some of the locals double up as extras in the series you may even recognise a few of them! The house used as the doctor's surgery is located a little way up Roscarrock Hill and the school house in Fore Street is a hotel and restaurant named the Old School. Other films and series such as the original *Poldark*, *Nightmare Man*, *Amy Foster* and *Saving Grace*, to name but a few have also been shot here. The interior designer Laurence Llewelyn-Bowen and his wife own a house and boutique in the village. There is an extremely narrow passageway in Port Isaac called Temple Bar but is appropriately nicknamed Squeeze-e-Belly Alley!

The small village quay is known as the Platt and fishermen's crab and lobster pots are still loaded and unloaded here, giving the whole place an authentic fishing village feel. It's wonderful to just soak up the atmosphere, especially with a pasty, a crab sandwich or an ice cream. What with the barnacle encrusted pots, a huge old rusty anchor and a menacingly threatening old World War II naval gun, the Platt is certainly a place in which to just watch the world go by. It's from here that the Port Isaac choir Fishermen's Friends began performing sea shanties and visitors may even be lucky enough to see one of their concerts. Many years ago a body was discovered dumped in a wheelbarrow near the Platt and ever since the actual site has been known as Bloody Bones Yard. Cars are allowed to park in neat rows on the beach but their stay is limited by the state of the tide. It's quite common to see cars stranded by the tide and occasionally even floating about. There are caves in the cliffs but beware getting caught out by the incoming tide. The 18th century Golden Lion inn apparently contains a secret smugglers' tunnel that once led through to one of the beach caves. There is a small aquarium nearby housed in the old pilchard sheds. As the 1987 book by Rosamunde Pilcher *The Shell Seekers* was partly filmed here in 2006 for a television mini-series version starring Vanessa Redgrave, it's a great place to relax and read it. The Porthkerris referred to in the book was depicted in the film as Port Isaac and although there is a real Porthkerris on Lizard Peninsular, it's widely believed that Rosamunde Pilcher may have actually had St Ives in mind for the Cornish part of the story.

Nearby Port Quin, or Porth Gwynn in Cornish meaning white cove, consists of just a few holiday cottages, which are all that now remain of 'the village that died'. A tale is told that in the 1800s all the men of the village were drowned whilst out fishing and so Port Quin soon became deserted. Another story blames navy press gangs. However the decline of the port's slate trade due to the coming of the railway is the more likely cause of its sad demise. A little further on is Doyden Castle, a 19th century folly built for Samuel Symmons in around 1830 so that he and his friends could drink and gamble there. It was even featured at the dramatic end of the 2011 series of *Doc Martin* and is nowadays a National Trust holiday let property. The remains of an Iron Age fort can be seen at the Rumps Peninsula, said to be the finest example in the whole of Cornwall. On the cliff top there, near Pentire Head, poet and artist Laurence Binyon wrote his well-known poem *For The Fallen* in 1914, part of which is recited throughout Britain on Remembrance Sunday.

PADSTOW

Padstow has been described as Cornwall's premiere destination, the food capital of Cornwall and often referred to as 'Padstein'. Padstow took its name from St Petrock who came over from Ireland in AD 518 and then later from St Patrick. Stowe means a holy place and the name Padstow is a corruption of its Saxon name Petrockstowe. In Cornish Padstow is known as Lannwedhenek (formally Lodenek) and is synonomous with the wonderfully talented chef Rick Stein. Padstow is the base of his seafood empire and former 1975 nightclub venture, with restaurants, cafes, B&B's, hotels, a renowned seafood school, a fishmongers, a deli, patisserie, shops, an excellent chip shop, etc to his name. He's even involved with the convivial Cornish Arms pub in nearby Churchtown, St Merryn and the empire is rapidly spreading!

Padstow has a wonderful active fishing harbour and a horseshoe of shops surrounds it. Back in 1890 the town was described in a guidebook as 'a mean-looking place of woe-begone aspect that no one would deliberately visit for its own sake'. Thankfully this description is now completely contradicted by the many smart shops, cafes, pubs, restaurants and all sorts of places, giving the impression that it's a vibrant, wealthy, chique location. Raleigh House (or Court House) by South Quay is of interest as it's where Sir Walter Raleigh (1552-1618) collected certain dues and payable taxes in his role as Warden of the Stannaries of Cornwall (1585-1603). At North Quay is located the oldest house in Padstow, namely the medieval Abbey House, which dates from the late 1400s. St Petroc's church in Treverbyn Road has an amazing medieval bench end carving depicting a fox giving a sermon to a congregation of geese.

During the Dark and Middle Ages missionaries and pilgrims once used the Saints Way (Forth an Syns), a 30-mile cross-country footpath to Fowey. Also known as the Drover's (or Pilgrim's) Way, this ancient medieval trade route, though some say it's possibly Bronze Age, eventually became overgrown and abandoned until its fortuitous re-discovery and subsequent re-establishment back in 1986. Rather than go by sea round Land's End, pilgrims and traders from such places as Wales and Ireland travelled cross-country on their way through to Europe and beyond. Locally there is a very popular part of the Cornish Way cycle path, which uses miles of the old Atlantic Coast Express railway track, known as the Camel Trail. There are superb beaches towards the mouth of the Camel estuary at nearby St George's Cove, Harbour Cove (Tregirls) and Hawker's Cove. The River Camel derives its name from *camhayle*, which is old Cornish meaning crooked or bent shaped estuary. In 1842 Charles Dickens met a Dr. Marley in Padstow and the good doctor's name became the inspiration for the surname of the character Jacob Marley in Dickens's famous 1843 tale, *A Christmas Carol*.

May Day is enthusiastically celebrated here annually. The Obby 'Oss (Hobby Horse) is one of the oldest surviving customs in Britain, if not in Europe and the inhabitants go wild for it. In the traditional *Cornish May Carol* song, keenly sung throughout Padstow on the day, there is another part known as the night song, which is sung at the stroke of midnight when April 30th becomes May 1st. It's used to wake anyone in Padstow who is asleep and kicks off the May Day celebrations in earnest. At 10am the day song and main celebrations take over and last all day and well into the night. There are in fact two Osses, the Old Oss whose supporters wear red and the Blue Ribbon Oss formally called the Temperance Oss and after World War I briefly known as the Peace Oss, whose followers obviously wear blue. In times past there were several Osses involved, although why horses nobody really knows anymore, as it's supposedly concerned with fertility rites. The place heaves with visitors and locals alike, all eager to join in the festivities and celebrate the first day of summer. In part it's reminiscent of the ancient festivities that also take place at Helston. Some say it all originates from ancient

Celtic pagan festivities for the return of the sun god Bel, others from the Gaelic festival of Beltane.

On South Quay is situated the National Lobster Hatchery (est 2000), which is a charitable organisation where lobsters are hatched, looked after and grown until they are released into the sea. The hatchery has carried out this procedure with many thousands of baby lobsters and local fishermen play their part too. They catch lobsters to sell for the pot but also donate some females with eggs, known as berries, to the hatchery, in order to further research and ultimately boost the lobster population. Their maternity ward is always very busy! If they find an unusual specimen, that too is donated, such as Jaffa, the one in ten million orange coloured lobster. There have also been examples of yellow, white, red, bright blue, calico (mottled) and split coloured live lobsters being found, when their usual colour is a dark reddish brown with some blue. For a small fee, baby lobsters can be adopted and individually named. Founded in 1971 the Padstow Museum (free entry) is housed in the former Men's Institute in Market Place and although small it's packed full of interest. A must to visit is the Elizabethan manor house, Prideaux Place (1592). For a 'pint of Padstow' try the tasty offerings of the Padstow Brewery Company (est 2013).

Padstow Bay is vast and tree stumps can occasionally be seen at very low tide. The Doom Bar sandbank is aptly named as many ships have been wrecked on it; visible if the tide is out, but once submerged can be lethal to shipping. The name Doom Bar is derived not from its deadly effect but from the old Cornish word *dun*, literally meaning in this case, hill of sand. Even nowadays mariners still need to heed the words of the old rhyme: 'From Padstow Point to Hartland Light, is a watery grave by day or night'. Legend has it that a mermaid created the Doom Bar when a local man apparently tried to kill her using a bow and arrow. To avenge the youth she threw a handful of sand into the sea and cursed both it and the area. Rock is only a stone's throw away from Padstow, both being situated on the Camel Estuary. In Cornish Rock is known as Karrek, however the village is badly named really as its beaches are actually sandy. The local quarry where ship's ballast was once excavated has long since closed and is now a busy car park. A frequent passenger ferry service operates throughout the year between Rock and Padstow. House prices in Rock are indeed far from rock-bottom, in fact it's one of the country's most expensive places to buy property, being often referred to as Chelsea-on-Sea, the Kensington of Cornwall and even Britain's Saint-Tropez. It's an affluent area where more millionaires live than anywhere else in Cornwall. The Camel Estuary is also an attractive proposition for wild salmon and otters that thrive in the clean waters. Sharp's Brewery was established in Rock back in 1994 and is home to brews such as Cornish Coaster, Doom Bar Bitter, Eden Ale and Chalky's Bite, named after Rick Stein's small terrier dog Chalky.

Close to Rock is St Enodoc's church in nearby Trebetherick, often invaded by sand and in the past spent over 200 years completely submerged beneath it. It has an amazingly twisted thirteenth-century spire, which was straightened in 1989 but not completely. The claim to fame of this 'golf course' church is it's the final resting place of the world famous poet Sir John Betjeman (1906-1984). He was made Poet Laureate in 1972, had a house nearby and even wrote about the area. The Jesus Well of Minver is located in the vicinity. Wadebridge hosts the three-day Royal Cornwall Show, held annually in early June at the showground located a mile to the west of Wadebridge on the A39. Wadebridge is known as Ponsrys in Cornish and was originally simply known as Wade until the construction of a bridge in 1468. In Cornish it's known as Ponswad. Wadebridge is also home to the John Betjamin Centre (1991), which is housed in an old railway station (free display in the memorabilia room) and the Wadebridge Folk Festival (or Cornish Folk Festival) held annually in August. Just off the A39 road at Tredinnick, near St Issey, is the Camel Creek Adventure Park, a fun packed venue for the whole family. At St Eval can be found the St Eval Kart Racing Circuit, with Go Karts to suit all ages and levels of experience.

BODMIN

The old stannary town of Bodmin is known as the Monk's town and in Cornish is Bosvena, meaning dwelling or house of the monks. Its patron saint is St Petroc and he established a small Benedictine monastery here in the 6th century. Bodmin has also been known as Petrockstow in the past. St Petroc's church at Athelstan Park is the largest in Cornwall and well worth inspection. St Guron's Well can be found in the churchyard and it was St Guron who first established a local hermitage resulting in Bodmin's location and development. The Bodmin Courtroom Experience takes place at Shire Hall, Mount Folly. The building dates back to about 1837 and was formally an old courtroom. Visitors can take part in a re-enactment of the trial of local boy, Matthew Weeks, who was accused of the murder of local girl, Charlotte Dymond, on Bodmin Moor in 1844. There is a memorial to her up at Rough Tor Ford and she is buried at Davidstow. In the courtroom visitors have to decide if Matthew Weeks was guilty of the murder and if he should hang for the offence or not. Nearby Bodmin Jail (Gaol) was built in 1778, closed in 1927 and now makes for a fascinating if rather macabre visit. Many prisoners were hung there in the past and the hanging pit is gruesomely displayed. During WWI the Domesday Book and the Crown Jewels were securely stored at the jail for safety reasons. John Arnold, inventor and watchmaker, was born in Bodmin in 1736. He became famous for making fine, accurate, portable timepieces, especially marine chronometers and was watchmaker to King George III.

The award winning Chapel an Gansblydhen (Centenary Chapel) Wetherspoon's pub on Fore Street was converted in 2008 from an old Wesleyan Methodist Chapel built in 1840 and has been lovingly restored, complete with church organ and pews! The Bodmin & Wenford Railway boasts a 13 mile round trip on a steam train and two museums worth visiting are the Bodmin Town Museum located at Mount Folly (free admission) and, just out of town, the Duke of Cornwall's Light Infantry Regimental Barracks Museum (est

1925). A walk up to the tall Gilbert Monument (1857) on Beacon Hill affords excellent views of the local area and Bodmin Beacon Nature Reserve (est 1994). A little further afield is Pencarrow House (1765) set in 50 acres of attractive gardens. A must to visit is nearby Lanhydrock House, being mostly Victorian, although there still exists a wonderful 17th century gatehouse. The infamous Jamaica Inn at Bolventor is another must see and seems likely to have derived its name from a powerful local family of landowners, two of whom became Governors of Jamaica during the 1700s. Once an old coaching inn, it was built in 1750 and frequented by many a villain. It's now much enlarged, has a museum dedicated to smuggling and Daphne du Maurier (see 77) and claims to be haunted. Between 1964 and 1976 the writer Alistair MacLean owned the inn. Both the inn and Bodmin Moor were the inspiration for Daphne du Maurier's novel, *Jamaica Inn* (1936) and therefore provide the most perfect setting to actually relax and enjoy reading it. Bodmin Moor used to be known as Foweymore and with all its bleakness is well worth exploring, with Rough Tor (Goen Bren) and Brown Willy (Bronn Wennili) being very popular. Rough Tor is pronounced 'Rau Tor'.

Of special interest are the many standing stones such as the Hurlers at Minions, numerous burial chambers such as Trethevy Quoit near St Cleer and natural features such as the Cheesewring Tor and also at Minions but beware of the infamous 'Beast of Bodmin'. It's apparently a species of large wild cat, perhaps a panther, said to terrorise the area and kill sheep and other animals. A visit to the legendary Dozmary Pool (formally Dozmare Pool) is highly recommended and is located close to Jamaica Inn. This is the mysterious site where Excalibur, the magical sword of King Arthur, is said to have been finally disposed of. The area is certainly atmospheric and one can easily imagine the hand of the 'Lady of the Lake' rising up to take Excalibur down to the depths below. The lake is glacial in origin and is in fact the only natural inland lake in Cornwall. Legend has it that the waters are bottomless but the droughts of 1859 and 1976 disproved that. Many Mesolithic,

Neolithic and Bronze Age artefacts have been found in and around Dozmary Pool, including flint arrowheads, flakes, cores, scrapers, knives and axes. For the legend of Tregeagle at Dozmary Pool refer to Porthleven (see 64). The pool's unusual name may stem from the Cornish *tos mery*, meaning pleasant drinking bowl, although others believe it to be from *doz mere*, meaning a drop of the sea. Not far away from Bodmin is the charming village of St Neot where they celebrate Oak Apple Day on May 29th. The church and its medieval stained glass windows are a delight. In the churchyard are to be found some fine examples of ancient Cornish crosses. Nearby is St Neot's Holy Well. The Carnglaze Caverns at St Neot are vast underground voids created from quarrying slate; wondrous to behold, they even host weddings and concerts.

NEWQUAY

Newquay is known as the capital of British surfing and is sometimes lovingly referred to as Surf City UK. In Cornish it's known as Tewynblustri meaning boat cove in the sand hills. The 'new' quay of Newquay was built in the 16th century to replace the old one of 1305, so it's not really that new anymore and in 1830 a new harbour was built. Newquay used to be written as New Quay. Many of Cornwall's beaches are great for surfing but Newquay is the undisputed centre of not just Cornish but of British surfing and it boasts eleven beaches and seven miles of sand. The main beaches are Fistral, which is of international surfing standard and easily the most famous surfing beach in Cornwall and the UK (great for families too), Towan, Great Western, Tolcarne and Lusty Glaze but there are quite a few others such as Watergate and Crantock. Once famous for pilchards, now shoals of surfers head to Newquay instead. There's a famous giant wave that occasionally forms here, namely the renowned and rare Cribber, which forms off the Cribber reef. This huge 20-30 foot monster wave is the ultimate dream of every surfer to conquer and is nicknamed the widow-maker for obvious reasons. The Cribbar pub located in Grover Lane is named after this infamous wave. Also look out for Rick Stein's restaurant at Fistral Beach.

Surfers are very keen on the SAS and with good reason. This is not the crack army squad however but the initials of the Surfers Against Sewage campaign. It speaks for itself really as they want to float about in clean water not in effluent. Ironically the word fistral (as in Fistral Beach) comes from the Cornish *porth an vystel*, meaning cove of the foul water, although this is actually in reference to the strong waves being unsuitable for landing boats. Surfers are certainly a dedicated bunch seemingly living off pure adrenalin most of the time. Apparently you have to be brave, fit, focused and optionally hunky, bronzed and young. They hit the surf whatever the weather, even in rarely seen snow! A demonstration of stand-up surfing was given in Newquay as far back as 1928 by Australian Olympian Charles Justin 'Snow' McAllister, the 'father' of Australian surfing. Bude claims to be the home of British surfing as the sport was established there in the 1940's but it's a contentious point around here.

The annual Newquay Fish Festival takes place in September and is one of the town's most prestigious events, including cooking demonstrations, stalls, beach games, boat rides, bands and real ale. William Golding, author of *Lord of the Flies* (1954) was born here in 1911 and the Roald Dahl's book *The Witches* was made into a film in 1990 at the local, highly impressive and award winning Headland Hotel. Towan Blystra (est 2003), the Wetherspoon's pub on Cliff Road gets its name from the anglicised name for the 1305 New Key, from the Cornish Tewynplustri. The railway journey from Newquay to Par is known as the Atlantic Coast Line and along its scenic miles of track a Real Ale Trail has cleverly been set up. Passengers can get on and off the train whenever and wherever they wish. Another railway attraction is the narrow gauge Lappa Valley Steam Railway located at St Newlyn East, established in 1974. There is also the Newquay Road Land Train (Surf Rider Train) service, consisting of a 45 minute loop road trip based in the town centre at Bank Street. It's a great alternate bus service, especially to the zoo, even if its American appearance is rather incongruous. An all-day ticket is cheaply available. Newquay Zoo (est 1969), located at Trenance Gardens, is the largest zoo in Cornwall and is well worth a visit, as is the Blue Reef Aquarium (est 2001) on Towan Promenade. In early summer lookout for the annual (free) Polo on the Beach weekend competition (est 2007) held at Watergate Bay and for the Pirate's Quest (est 2015) experience at 22 St Michael's Road for an interactive swashbuckling adventure!

Close by is Towan Island (or The Island), complete now with a self-catering luxury Unique Home Stays house perched on the summit and dubbed 'the House in the Sea'. It's joined to the mainland by a private footbridge precariously suspended 80ft in the air. The house was originally built in 1901 and was once owned by the inventor Alexander Lodge (1881-1938) who helped to develop the spark plug. Sir Arthur Conan Doyle (1859-1930) often visited this wonderful house, which could well have been the inspiration for *The Lost World* (1912) and perhaps even developed, amongst others, some of his later Sherlock Holmes stories here. The old whitewashed Huer's Hut perched above the harbour on Towan Head, not far from the Red Lion Inn on North Quay Hill, is now an historic listed building but in bygone years it was a look-out point to inform the local fishermen when shoals of pilchards were present in the bay (see 13). This intriguing stone building is also known as the Huer's House and is thought to have originally been a fourteenth century hermitage, complete with medieval chimney. In those days the hut would have acted as a navigational beacon at night when a visible fire would have been lit to aid shipping. Currently there is no access to the inside of the building. Back in 1967 the Beatles once frolicked on the beach at Watergate Bay as they filmed *Magical Mystery Tour*. Jamie Oliver has his Fifteen Cornwall restaurant here, built in 2006 with stunning views for its customers to enjoy, as well as excellent cuisine. Newquay is a vibrant town that welcomes responsible visitors and any excess energy can always be channelled into the medieval sport of Cornish wrestling, which also has judo mixed into it somehow, as the tradition still flourishes here.

At Tresillian Barton can be found the Dairyland Farm World, a Cornish Heritage Museum (est 1975), an adventure playground, a nature trail, a huge undercover play area and much more besides. Trerice House at Kestle Mill is a small Elizabethan manor house constructed in 1571. Near to Newquay is the curiously named village of Porth Joke, also known as Polly Joke, its name possibly derived from the Cornish for Jackdaw Cove, namely Porth Jouack (or Porth Chauk). Not far from Newquay is Holywell and the Holywell Bay Fun Park (free entry). The Screech Owl Sanctuary (est 1990) at Goss Moor, St Columb, is another popular visitor attraction, where injured and sick owls can be seen being cared for and rehabilitated. Founded by a Mr and Mrs Screech, there is actually an owl species named the Screech owl! Also at St Columb is the Cornish Birds of Prey Centre (est 2007), Winnards Perch. The infamous John Trehenban was born in St Columb in 1650 and at the age of 21 was convicted of the murder of two young girls. His sentence was to be confined in a cage on the downs of nearby Iron Age hillfort Castle an Dinas and starved to death within it. It's said that a stone still on the hilltop today is the actual one on which the cage (or gibbet) once stood. His body would have been left there on 'display' for several years to act as a gruesome deterrent to others contemplating such a heinous crime.

Newquay Airport is located at nearby St Mawgan and serves such places as the Isles of Scilly (see 58), London, Edinburgh, Manchester, Italy and Düsseldorf. It has one of the longest runways in Great Britain at nearly two miles in length. For a fun time try out your co-ordination skills on an electric, self-balancing 'scooter' transporter at the Cornwall Segway centre at nearby Hendra Holiday Park. Located at nearby Crantock Beach more or less below the Crantock Bay Hotel is a small tidal cave sometimes referred to as Lady Cave, which lies to the left hand side of the beach, in Piper's Hole and therein lies a sad story. On the wall is carved a large portrait of a woman, a heart-rending section of verse and the small outline of a horse. It's the artistic work of Joseph Prater, whose love went out riding across the sands but sadly got cut off by the rising tide and both she and her horse were tragically drowned. This all happened in the early 1900s but the carving and wording is clear. The village of Crantock itself is named after St Carantocus and the present Norman church of St Carantoc is dedicated to this sixth century Welsh saint. In Cornish the village is known as Lanngorrow (Langurroc) meaning the dwelling of monks. If crossing the estuary ford of the River Gannel by foot between Newquay and Crantock, take heed not only of the extremely dangerous tides but also of the guttural shriek of the ghostly Gannel Crake that allegedly haunts the area and foretells death. Some would rather take the long five-mile inland detour rather than risk such a crossing. Doubters say it's merely the wind blowing along the estuary or perhaps just the call of the rare corncrake but take heed nevertheless, as many people have actually lost their lives there by drowning. Is it more than just coincidence that during the time of the Black Death in Bodmin (1349), around one and a half thousand victims were brought from there and buried on mass in a local coastal field?

PERRANPORTH

Perranporth is an old 19th century tin mining town and has been described as a saintly place to visit in original 'Poldark' country. The Cornish name Porthperan means St Piran's cove and St Piran, the patron saint of Cornwall, came over from Ireland many centuries ago and landed in the cove. St Piran created an oratory (chapel) to preach from, which is still preserved to this day in the local sand dunes and a memorial stone now marks the site. This sixth century building is sometimes referred to as the lost church and is said to be the oldest Christian church in Britain. It was first unearthed in 1835 and is now scheduled for excavation and preservation. The remains of a later church (referred to as St Piran's old church) built around 1150 are located nearby, with the church being abandoned in 1795 and demolished in 1804.

Perranporth boasts the magnificent Perran Beach and the local cliffs include some impressive rock arches that are destined to become stacks in the not too distant geological future. The power of the sea to erode the rock to such an extent is remarkable. Dead Man's Cave is rather eerie and high above one part of the cliff, to the left of the most prominent arch, is a man-made entrance to a small cave or chapel that had been carved out of solid rock. It's easy to imagine a solitary pilgrim or monk living a hermit's life there, perhaps even St Piran himself. Close to this prominent arch is Chapel Rock. At Cligga Head wolfram was formally mined to make nitro-glycerine for the Alfred Nobel explosives factory there. He invented dynamite in 1867 and after his death in 1896 his wealth funded the Nobel Peace Prize institute. Perranporth is a mellow place for people and is especially popular with families, surfers and dog owners. Dogs are welcome on the beach here all year round (but kept on leads during July and August between 9:30 am-5:00 pm) although this is not always the case elsewhere along the Cornish coast. Dog owners need to check very carefully if there are any restrictions beforehand, as they range throughout coastal Cornwall from dogs welcome all year, to dogs absolutely not welcome and banned from certain beaches. Incidentally, many pubs in Cornwall allow entry to well-behaved dogs on leads.

Although Perranporth has superb surfing, care needs to be taken as it has very strong rip tides. The lifeguards use a system of warning flags to aid those in the water. Black and white flags mean don't swim there as surfers and boats use the area. Red and yellow flags mean it's safe to swim there and that lifeguards patrol it. An orange windsock tells everyone it's dangerously windy and that nobody is allowed to go into the sea with inflatable lilos and such. Finally a red flag stands for danger and that the water should not be entered and if in it there is a need to get out fast. Back in the 1920s coffin maker Tom Tremewan used coffin lids as the first UK surfboards although they were just referred to as boards back then and places like Bude and Newquay eventually copied the idea. In 1898 the car designer Donald Healey was born in Perranporth, his name forever linked with the Austin Healey and the Austin Healey

Sprite. He opened a local garage and in 1931 won the Monte Carlo Rally. The five day Lowender Peran (Festival of the Celts) is held in October and celebrates Cornwall's Celtic links and heritage. Perranporth's giant Millennium sundial stands proud on the top of the hill at Droskyn Point, above the nearby rock arches, on the site of the old Droskyn Mine. It's designed round Cornish Natural Time rather than Greenwich Mean Time, thus being 20 minutes slower, due to the sun rising and setting 20 minutes later in Cornwall than it does in London.

Almost every coastal village and town in Cornwall lays claim to the first *Poldark* television series being filmed there in the 1970s but actually Winston Mawdsley Graham (1908-2003) wrote the first novel *Ross Poldark* back in 1945 while actually living in Perranporth. He had moved down from Manchester in 1925 at the age of 17. Graham also wrote the next three books in the series of twelve whilst still living in Perranporth, namely *Demelza* (1946), *Jeremy Poldark* (1950) and *Warleggan* (1953). The BBC finally acknowledged his historical novels when actor Robin Ellis played hero Ross Poldark in the original TV adaptation. This turbulent costume drama all about tin mines, greed, relationships, love and such ran on the BBC for almost 30 episodes between 1975 and 1977. The popular BBC 2015 television remake of the series starring Aiden Turner was filmed in such Cornish locations as Charlestown Harbour, Porthcothan (as Nampara Cove), Gunwallow Church Cove (shipwreck scenes), Pedn Vounder (beach scenes), Botallack Wheal Owles and Wheal Crowns (as part of Wheal Leisure), Levant Mine (as Tressider's Rolling Mill), Porthgwarra, St Agnes Head (as Nampara Valley), St Breward (as Nampara House and miner's cottages), Bodmin Moor and Poldark Mine itself (underground scenes and general mining artefacts).

Entry is free to the Perranzabuloe Museum (est 1985), which is located in Oddfellows Hall, Ponsmere Road. The Green Parrot pub (est 2010) is located in Hanover Close, St Georges Hill, the only pub in the UK completely surrounded by beach. This welcome oasis is located on Perran Beach and is dog friendly. There are some wonderful ciders to choose from at Healey's Cornish Cyder Farm at nearby Penhallow (free entry), home of Rattler cyder, Cyder Brandy and Fruit Liquors.

ST AGNES

St Agnes has been described as a giant of a place. It's named after Agnes, a first century Roman saint and in Cornish is known as Breanek meaning pointed hill or beacon of Agnes. There are plenty of old engine houses known as Cornish Castles and the spoil heaps of numerous tin mines. They litter the landscape and are ghostly reminders of an era long since departed. In 1763 the two-masted brigantine ship *Hanover* sank at nearby Hanover Cove on its return from Lisbon to Falmouth, with only three survivors out of the 67 on board. The cove was thus named in the ship's honour. Its cargo of cannons and gold bullion was valued at 15 million pounds and most, though not all, was recovered. Located in the heart of the village down Town Hill at the back of St Agnes Parish Church is a steep row of nine terraced cottages (1840s). These are situated in a lane curiously named Stippy Stappy (formally Cottage Row and Boatman's Row), which even gets a mention in Winston Graham's Poldark novels. They were originally owned and rented out by the Trevaunance (Cove) harbour managers to master mariners (sea captains) and sailors but in later years, as the harbour declined, local tin miners occupied them. Perhaps the name Stippy Stappy bears some descriptive reference to the incline of the rooftops and may have been derived from the expression 'steep step'.

The St Agnes Museum (est 1984, free admission) is housed in an old chapel of rest located in Penwinnick Road and makes for a worthwhile visit, as do the nearby Blue Hills Tin Stream mine at Wheal Kitty, the 1961 Veryan Defensive (Cold War) Bunker and the Driftwood Spars Hotel at Trevaunance Cove. The latter is a 17th century inn built using ships' timbers from local shipwrecks, the use of which gave the building its name. The Driftwood Spars Micro Brewery started business in the year 2000 in an old café opposite the hotel but ceased production in 2007 before starting up again with the introduction of Blue Hills Bitter and the clever idea of Furnace, an alcoholic ginger beer. At one time they introduced Cuckoo Ale, a name with a legend attached to it. Local men once believed that if they prevented the cuckoo from leaving St Agnes it would forever remain spring there. They built a high stone wall but sadly the bird escaped, although the legend remains and the brewery's label depicts the story. Another local brewery is the Hogswood Brewing Company (est 2009), located at Higher Goshen, Mithian. The artist John Opie was born at nearby Trevellas village in 1761; known as the Cornish Wonder, he was a member of the Royal Academy and upon his death in 1807 was buried in St Paul's Cathedral.

Yet another cuckoo legend here tells of a farmer who once threw a hollow log onto a fire one cold, dull April day. When a cuckoo flew out the weather instantly improved. From then on the locals held a Cuckoo Feast every April on the nearest Sunday to the 28th. Another legend related to St Agnes concerns the Giant Bolster who bled to death whilst trying to fill a hole in the rock with his own blood as a love token to St Agnes, who asked him to do it. He bled to death as the hole ran underground into the sea but the red staining of his 'blood' can still be seen in the rocks at Chapel Porth, where the deed took place. It's said that his ghost appears every spring searching for his beloved St Agnes. In reality the blood red staining is due to the presence of iron deposits in the local rocks. Tin streaming can be found at the Blue Hills Tin Streams, Wheal Kitty, on the outskirts of St Agnes, where tin is reclaimed from alluvial deposits by the use of water. It appears to be the only working tin streaming site in Cornwall, which is ironic considering the multitude there once were. At the site the age old tradition of extracting and smelting tin from local alluvial deposits before it's crafted into jewellery continues. The mine is open to visitors. Perranporth Aerodrome, located at Higher Trevellas, was built in 1941 for the RAF as a Spitfire station. St Agnes Head is a great place to view the night sky as it's been scientifically designated as a prestigious 'Dark Sky' area.

PORTREATH

The Cornish name for the village is Porthtreth meaning beach harbour. It has been described as a place bathed in history and the Basset family are at the heart of it all, there's even a Basset's Cove nearby. In the 1800s Lady Frances Basset's wealthy father had several bath-sized holes cut out in the rocks around the beach for her to bathe in refreshing, healing, salty sea water and they still exist today. Apparently the sand on Portreath beach contains particles of tin and gold and many years ago someone found enough gold to make a ring. A submerged forest is sometimes exposed on the beach after heavy storms and just off shore is Gull Rock, a much-photographed outcrop. There is a sad story connected with the area as the steamer *Escurial* sank in local waters in 1895 during a winter storm, with the result that eleven out of 18 crewmen lost their lives. The anchor from that ill-fated ship now rests outside the Portreath Arms Hotel in The Square, another sobering reminder of the merciless power of the sea.

The nearby Nancekuke military area was once a chemical warfare base with nerve gas apparently being a particular speciality but it cleaned its act up years ago and is now known as RAF Portreath, being connected with the more routine task of radar surveillance duties. Also nearby is Ralph's Cupboard, a place of legend as it's there that the giant known as Wrath of Portreath lived. He often attacked passing ships, eating the passengers and crew. Some vessels were tied by rope to his belt and pulled into his gigantic lair and he would also throw giant boulders at shipping as a warning to stay away and these are strewn around the local waters where they form a dangerous reef.

REDRUTH

In Cornish Redruth is Resrudh, meaning river ford of red. Originally Redruth grew around Church Town because of St Uny's Holy Well, the waters of which were supposed to stop anyone who drank them from ever being hanged. The well still exists and can be found close to Carn Brea village, not far below the beautiful church in Church Town, dedicated to St Uny, with its interesting 1490s built tower, Henry VII gargoyle and lych-gate dating from 1810. The natural granite beauty of Carn Brea Hill dominates the skyline for miles around and on its summit is Carn Brea Castle (1,379 ft) and also the Basset Monument erected in 1836 to the memory of Francis Basset, a major mine owner of the district. Traces of ancient earthworks litter the area amid legends of stone-throwing giants. There still exist plenty of old engine house ruins, lovingly referred to as Cornish castles, scattered throughout the Redruth area and especially at Carn Brea, where tin and copper mines once abounded. These engine houses were part of a thriving mining industry but are now just ghostly relics of former glory days. Winding engine houses brought up ore laden rock to the surface, pumping engine houses helped to rid the mines of unwanted underground water and stamp engine houses powered crushing machines, although some were purely water driven. There would have been huge spoil heaps, which together with all the associated mine buildings and related industry, would have made the area unrecognisable from what it is today. In places the landscape would have resembled an industrial war zone and some of the rivers even ran red with minerals (iron oxide), hence the origin of Redruth's name, although the miners likened it more to the blood spilt by miners of old.

There is an interesting large bronze statue in Fore Street that celebrates the town's heritage. It depicts a tin miner and was created by David Annand in 2008. There are also the controversial Tinner's Hounds (or Redruth Dogs) sculptures, which were cast by David Kemp in 2007 from old discarded tin miners' boots. Gas lighting was actually invented here in Redruth in 1792 by Scotsman William Murdock. He used the coal gas to illuminate his home, which still survives in Cross Street and he also made the first steam locomotive in 1784. A Murdock Day celebration is held here annually. The annual Redruth Cornish Pasty Festival is a three-day delight not to be missed! Drummer Mick Fleetwood of the world famous group Fleetwood Mac was born here in Redruth in 1947, as was comedian Rory McGrath in 1956. A fascinating book entitled *A Cornish Waif's Story* (1954, republished in 2010) was written by Mabel Carvolth who was born in Redruth Workhouse at Barncoose in 1894. It's an autobiography written under the pseudonym Emma Smith and depicts her harsh life as an illegitimate child abandoned by her mother. She soon found herself toiling at the age of five for an evil family and earned her keep by traipsing all over Cornwall singing and collecting money for them to earn her keep. She finally escaped her misery by running away at the age of twelve and sought sanctuary by joining a nunnery. In later life she attained normality with her loving husband Barney and a family of her own until her death in 1984 at the age of 89.

Nearby is Gwennap Pit, a grassy, open-air amphitheatre made famous by Methodist preacher John Wesley (1703-1791). It's man made and was first visited by him in 1762. Closely associated with the mining industry and Redruth is nearby Camborne, or in Cornish Cambron (Kammbronn), meaning crooked hill. The Camborne School of Mines in Pool was established in 1851 and the Camborne Geological Museum and Gallery is worth visiting, especially as admission is free. At Pool is also the East Pool Mine in Trevithick Road, which houses one of the largest surviving Cornish beam engines in the world. At Penponds village is the cottage that Richard Trevithick, inventor, engineer and steam locomotive pioneer, lived in as a child in the 1770s. It was built in 1700 and is now managed by the Trevithick Trust. Viewing is limited so check beforehand. Cornishman Richard Trevithick, known to many as Captain Dick, was born in 1771 in Carn Brea, Illogan, between Camborne and Redruth. He became an engineer at Penzance's Ding Dong mine and began tinkering around with steam engines, improved mine engines, invented the Cornish Boiler-Beam Engine, the 'Puffing Devil' road steam vehicle and also the steam locomotive 'Catch Me Who Can' that ran on rails. On Christmas Eve 1801 he undertook an epic steam engine ride in his road vehicle 'Puffing Devil' up Camborne Hill. The trial was a total success although the boiler blew up afterwards when Richard and friends were celebrating in a local hostelry. Good old Captain Dick had forgotten in the heat of the moment that boilers need water. His inventions went from strength to strength but lack of backing scuppered his wonderful plans. He died in 1833 and his life is celebrated in Camborne on Trevithick Day, which falls on the last Saturday of April. A statue in his honour graces a plinth outside Camborne library in Cross Street. He wouldn't recognise the modern railway system but it's all thanks to Richard Trevithick that we have one today and the much loved old song *Going up Camborne Hill (Coming Down)* is proudly and frequently sung in his memory.

Pool is also the site of the Heartlands Project which opened in 2012 and includes free cultural attractions such as botanical gardens, a huge adventure playground, various heritage exhibitions and craft studios. Set in 19 acres it's based at the Robinson's Shaft area of the former South Crofty Mine, Dundance Lane, Pool. Not far away from Redruth is the Shire Horse Farm and Carriage Museum at Lower Gryllis Farm, Treskillard. At Troon is the King Edward Mine Museum, now a mining World Heritage Centre. The Mineral Tramway Discovery Centre is a mine of information and admission is free. There are many walks and trails to take in this area and beyond, all having a mining theme, such as the Great Flat Lode Trail. Tolgus Mill on the New Portreath Road is a good place to see a former tin streaming mill, a rare survivor of a former age. The restored (2014) Giant's Quoit at Carwynnen is a Bronze Age Burial Chamber over five thousand years old and is certainly worth a visit. It's also locally known as the Carwynnen Quoit or by the nickname of the Devil's Frying Pan. The Doghouse Brewery (est 2003) is located in nearby Scorrier and the Wetherspoon's pub in Church Street, Camborne, named after John Francis Basset, was established in 2011 and is housed in the former Market House.

HAYLE

Hayle has been described as Cornwall's other Eden, a Cornish paradise and the cradle of the Industrial Revolution. It's known as

Heyl in Cornish, with *heyl* meaning estuary and is blessed with three miles of golden sand. The dunes are known locally as the Towans and during World War II an explosives factory was sited amongst them. Suzan Pierce Tadd was born in Hayle c1844 and her daughter, born in Canada as Florence Nightingale Graham later changed her name to Elizabeth Arden and founded her cosmetic empire in the USA. Rick Rescoria, who led nearly 3,000 people to safety following the World Trade Center terrorist attack in 2001, was also born here. Tragically he died trying to save even more lives and in honour of his courageous efforts a memorial was erected in his memory in 2002 at the harbour side. The Cornish Stannary Parliament honoured him with the White Cross of Cornwall as a tribute to his courage and bravery. The brilliant Paradise Park Wildlife Sanctuary (including Junglebarn) located in Trellissick Road houses the World Parrot Trust and is deeply involved with the Operation Chough project (see 16), is well worth a visit. Housed in John Harvey House at 24, Foundry Square, is located the Hayle Heritage Centre (free entry) established in 2013. In the nearby village of Lelant romantic novelist Rosamunde Pilcher was born in 1924 and books such as *The Shell Seekers* (1988) made her world famous. Godrevy Island has the impressive Godrevy Lighthouse (1859) firmly built upon it, providing the inspiration for Virginia Woolf's 1927 novel *To The Lighthouse*. A park and float ferry scheme (est 2014) between Hayle (North Quay) and St Ives provides a popular 'harbour taxi' shuttle service.

ST IVES

St Ives, known in Cornish as Porth Ia, has been described as being spectacular, charming and at the heart of Cornish art, with the Great Western Railway (GWR) even dubbing it the 'Naples of the West'. It's named after St Ia, a 5th/6th century female Irish saint whose well (Venton Ia) is located at the base of Porthmeor Hill and was given a granite make-over in around 1692. Until 1843 it was the area's main supply of drinking water. Over the years this old fishing port has grown in popularity, often voted the best place to live in the UK and the main pursuit of catching fish has mostly given way now to tourism. Artists have been attracted to St Ives and its luminescent, ethereal light, for decades and there certainly is something about the place that's unique and almost Mediterranean. It's a prestigious UK and European beach destination that can boast several pristine beaches including the wonderful Harbour Beach; the award winning Porthminster Beach, the name meaning beach of the church, which is situated below the railway station and the superb Porthmeor Beach below Tate St Ives, excellent for surfing. There is also the smaller Porthgwidden Beach meaning white cove in Cornish, referring to the colour of the sand. It's located adjacent to the headland 'Island' and tiny Bamaluz Beach, itself located between Smeaton's Pier and Porthgwidden Beach. Outside St Ives is nearby Carbis Bay (aka Porthrepta or Barrepta Cove), which boasts a white beach. The name Carbis stems from the Cornish word *karrbons*, meaning causeway. Porthrebtor means cove by the hill in Cornish, with Barrebtor meaning summit by the tor.

The Tate art gallery (Tate St Ives) opened in 1993 and was built on a former gasworks site, bringing with it the sweet smell of success and the whole town is heaving with artistic talent. Barbara Hepworth (1903-1975) adored the place and the Barbara Hepworth Museum & Sculpture Garden at Barnoon Hill are testament to this. The nearby Trewyn Subtropical Gardens is a charming, meditative place hidden away right in the heart of St Ives just off the High Street and along the lane behind Barclays Bank. It's considered by many locals to be the town's green lung and its secret garden. Bernard Leach (1887-1979) was also potty about St Ives and his pottery, founded in 1920, is now the Leach Museum and is dedicated to his talents as Britain's best-known studio potter. It's to be found outside St Ives at Higher Stennack. Not only were tin and copper once mined in the St Ives vicinity but also uranium rich pitchblende deposits at Trenwith Mine, used by Madame Curie herself as part of her ground-breaking research into radiation.

St Ives railway station and the views of the bay from the train are well worth the price of a return ticket to St Erth. The adjacent Malakoff bus depot has great views of the Island, which is really a small headland peninsula, being majestically crowned by St Nicholas's chapel, itself pre-15th century but sadly all but demolished in 1904 and subsequently rebuilt in 1911. In 1979 its roof was destroyed by a terrible storm and as part of the film *Raise The Titanic* (1980) was being shot on location around here at the time, the company paid for its restoration and switched to using nearby Barnoon Cemetery instead. The peninsula is known as Pendinnas, the Cornish for headland of the fortress and is often referred to as just the Island, a walk around which is recommended. The Malakoff area of St Ives takes its name from the 1855 Crimean Battle of Malakoff. Local children used to apparently re-enact the war scenes there.

The St Ives railway line was opened in 1877, which really opened the floodgates as far as tourism was concerned but it was threatened with closure in 1963 under the Beeching railway restructuring proposals. Opposition was strong and in order to support the case the music duo Flanders and Swann wrote the song *Slow Train* in 1963, which helped in the line's ultimate reprieve. A special railway journey from St Ives to Penzance is known as the St Ives Bay Line and along its scenic miles of track a Real Ale Trail has been set up. For the cost of a ticket passengers have full use of the railway and can get on and off the train whenever and wherever they wish, although they have to change at St Erth anyway to join the main line connection to Penzance. The beers of the St Ives Brewery (est 2010) are well worth seeking out and one brew, namely Boilers Golden Cornish Ale, takes its name from the 1938 wreck of the Panamanian steamer *Alba*, the rusted boilers of which are still visible at low tide on Porthmeor Beach. Five of the crew drowned in the disaster, which also resulted in the loss of the RNLI lifeboat. The Hain Steamship Company was established in St Ives in 1878 and when Edward Hain died in 1917 it was quickly purchased and combined with others to form the famous P&O Shipping Company. A Captain Sampson used to take pilchards to Ireland and bring back Guinness as part of a return deck cargo selling it in his 16th century local pub, the Skidden, located on Skidden Hill close to Street an Pol and now known as the Skidden House Hotel. Subsequently, with agreement from Arthur Guinness himself, it became the first establishment under licence to sell Guinness in the UK (circa 1760). The Hain Line Wetherspoon pub in Tregenna Place was established in 2012 and is built on the site of former office of the Hain Steamship Company. Ironically there is a local thoroughfare named Teetotal Street by the Temperance Society and close to it, housed in the old Seamen's Mission building, is the St Ives Museum (1924) at Wheal Dream, which is independently run, packed full of interest and a joy to visit.

In 1549 the Port Warden Customs Officer Portreeve John 'Tregenna' Payne was hanged in St Ives for using the newly prohibited Latin prayer book during Mass rather than the newly translated English Common Prayer Book version. Payne had been involved in the uprising and subsequent rebellious Exeter march against the religious changes brought about under the name of King Edward VI. Not only was he tricked into building his own gallows but also providing himself and accuser Provost Marshall Sir Anthony Kingston with a hearty meal just prior to the unexpected execution by lunching at the Old George & Dragon Inn (demolished 1887) in the Market Place. The hanging took place near the Golden Lion and the parish church of St Ia (also dedicated to St Peter & St Andrew, built 1426 or 1429), outside Market House, which was originally built in 1490 (rebuilt 1832) and is easily identified even today by its curved frontage. The church was a chapel of ease built in 1434 and only became a parish church in 1826. The Market Place is also where the old town stocks, lock-up cell and whipping post were located. These days a large granite War Memorial in the form of a Cornish Celtic cross can be seen and the adjacent Memorial Gardens are serenely beautiful and well worth viewing. In the church grounds is located a large and interesting medieval lantern cross. At the top of

Skidden Hill there's a wall plaque dedicated to John Payne's memory on the church wall of the Sacred Heart & St Ia (1908). In the late 1930s, before the onset of World War II, high-ranking Nazi official Joachim Von Ribbentrop, Adolf Hitler's right-hand man, regularly visited St Ives and apparently held it in high esteem.

The lantern lit ghost story walk consists of more than an hours worth of visiting the darker side of St Ives and being scared witless into the bargain. One of the chilling stories told concerns the 'Lady with the Lantern'. Many years ago she was found struggling in the waters of a shipwreck with her baby held safely in her arms but by the time she was lifted to the safety of a nearby boat her baby was missing, presumed dead. The lady was so grief stricken that she too died and it's said that her ghostly image can sometimes seen searching for the baby on the local rocks and shoreline. The ghostly spectre carries a lantern when it's dark and to observe this apparition is apparently an omen of forthcoming doom. There are other ghost stories and strange goings on in and around St Ives, like the spectre that rides a ghostly white horse, the ghosts of drowned sailors and murder victims, weird howling or whistling noises such as the Seven Whistlers, the ghostly sight of gallows victim John Payne and strange lights in the sky such as the red glow of Jack Harry's Lights. Seeing or hearing any of these is said to bring bad luck to the observer. Keep a mindful eye on the skies hereabouts as apparently the 'Cornwall Unidentified Flying Object (UFO) Triangle' stretches from St Ives as far as Land's End and the Falmouth area! Look out for a tall, pointed granite obelisk on the skyline beyond the railway station as it's actually Mayor John Knill's Steeple. It was meant to be his mausoleum but he died in London in 1811 so was never buried beneath it. He was also a Customs Officer and it's said that this structure on Worvas Hill was also built as a good navigation aid for smugglers, with whom Knill was not averse to having lucrative dealings with. Every five years on July 25th (St James' Day) a ceremony takes place in his honour. The first such occasion took place in 1801 when John Knill himself joined in with the festivities.

After the 2016 ceremony, the next will take place in 2021.

There is a real feel of history to St Ives. There are quaint little alleys all over the place and the sea is never far away. Smeaton's Pier, built in 1767 by John Smeaton, architect of the Eddystone Lighthouse, is well worth seeing close up and seals are regular visitors to the harbour. Beyond the old lookout lighthouse (1831) on Smeaton's Pier, an extension named Victoria Pier was built in 1890, complete with yet another lookout lighthouse and as it's made from cast iron it often appears rather rusty. Nearby look out for the remains of the old wooden pier (1865) and note the three arches in Smeaton's Pier cleverly added in 1890 to combat harbour silting; apparently they were rather too efficient and had to be partly blocked off to avoid small boats being dislodged from their moorings.

Just before the start of Smeaton's Pier is located the medieval (pre 1577) St Leonard's Chapel for fishermen, who before sea trips would celebrate mass here and the chaplain would receive a cut of the catch as payment. In 1971 it was converted into a small mini museum dedicated to the memory of St Ives fishermen and is a very sparse, contemplative building. Along Wharf Road at the other end of Harbour Beach is the much smaller West Pier, which was constructed in 1894 and is the location of the St Ives Lifeboat Station, which in 1939 lost seven brave members of its crew from the *John and Sarah Eliza Stych*, who were tragically drowned out in the bay whilst going to the help of others in distress. The annual St Ives Art and Literature September Festival is a popular event and another crowd puller in the depths of winter is the St Ives traditional ceremony of the Hurling of the Silver Ball, which takes place in February. No sticks are involved, just plenty of throwing. The ancient Sloop Inn is a pub steeped in history and was apparently built in c1312, thus making it one of oldest pubs in Cornwall. The Porthgwidden Beach Café is highly recommended, as is a boat trip to Seal Island.

ZENNOR

Zennor is named after St Senara and in Cornish is known as Eglossenar, with *eglo* meaning church. Zennor is yet another Cornish village with a wonderful legend attached to it. Apparently there was a strange woman who frequented the local church, St Senara's (rebuilt 12th century, pre 1150) and was always garbed in long flowing skirts. Where she lived was unknown. Eventually local lad Matthew Trewhella married her and after visiting nearby Vear Cove they were never seen again, not on land anyway. Local fishermen occasionally still speak of melodic voices serenading a watery crèche. In the church on an old 15th century bench-end that has evolved into a seat is a carving depicting the mermaid, a rather unusual item for a religious building. John Davey the younger (1812-1891) was buried in Zennor churchyard in 1891. He was considered the last Cornishmen who could not only read and speak his mother tongue Kernowek but also had extensive knowledge of it. Hence Zennor is considered one of the last bastions of the Cornish language. Also born in the churchyard in 1857 is Henry Quick, known as the Zennor (or peasant) poet and born in the village in 1792.

The 1961 horror film *Doctor Blood's Coffin* was filmed in these parts. There is also the legend of the red cat of Zennor which concerns a lady who wanted for some unknown reason to breed tigers. The powers that be denied her and so she vowed instead to breed cats that were as ferocious as tigers. Certain cats in the district are said to have a reddish-orange tinge to their fur and are thus presumed fierce. The local Tinners Arms pub dates from around 1271 and its main claim to fame is that the author D.H. Lawrence (1885-1930) stayed in the pub and around Zennor during 1916 and 1917. He wrote *Women in Love* (1920) in nearby Higher Tregerthen. His first wife Frieda was German and due to anti-German feelings at the time and the fact that everyone thought they had been signalling to enemy submarines, the couple were eventually asked by the local constabulary to leave Cornwall. One of Frieda's relatives was the Red Baron, the famous German fighter pilot ace Manfred von Richthofen, who piloted a distinctive red Fokker tri-plane. D.H. Lawrence's general Cornish experiences were written about in his book *Kangaroo* (1923) and even Frieda Lawrence wrote about it in her 1935 autobiography. There's a Stone Age tomb at Zennor Quoit and the Wayside Museum in Zennor (est 1930s) is apparently the oldest privately owned museum in Britain, housed inside twelve themed and undercover areas within the grounds of Trewey Mill. Look out for the tasty Moomaid (of Zennor) ice cream, which is made at nearby Tremedda Farm.

PENDEEN

Pendeen in Cornish is Boskaswal Wartha meaning the headland of a fort. Pendeen Watch (Penn Din) is the location of the now unmanned Pendeen lighthouse (est 1900), which safely watches over the area. Pendeen house is where the Cornish historian Reverend Dr. William Borlase (1695-1772) was born. Geevor Tin Mine on the outskirts of Pendeen is very evocative of Cornwall's mining heritage and is in fact the largest preserved mining location in Great Britain. It closed as a working mine in 1990, re-opened in 1993 as Cornwall's premier mining centre and is an award winning attraction that's well worth seeing. There are many abandoned mines throughout the area and engine house 'castles' are dotted around like something out of a scene from the potteries. The word Geevor is possibly derived from the Cornish word *gever* meaning nanny goat, hence the mining company's symbol was that of a goat, although unusually it has a symbolic fish tail replacing the back half of its body, as in the commonly used depiction of the astrological sign of the zodiac representing Capricorn, namely the mythical sea-goat.

ST JUST

St Just is simply named after Saint Just and in Cornish is known as Lannust. It's the most westerly town in Cornwall, having at its centre a medieval theatre site known as Plain-an-Gwarry, which was used to enact miracle plays. The Lafrowda Festival (est 1996) is held here annually and is a popular summer event of art and culture. The nearby coastal ruins of the Botallack mine buildings are a popular tourist attraction. Nearby Cape Cornwall is often known as the connoisseurs Land's End and is apparently the only designated cape in Cornwall, England and Wales. In 1987 Heinz, the company of baked beans fame, gave Cape Cornwall to the National Trust in celebration of their centenary and a monument was erected to commemorate the occasion. At nearby Kelynack is the private base of Land's End Airport, from where short flights can be taken to the Isles of Scilly (see 58).

LAND'S END

Land's End has been described as a legendary destination. It's known in Cornish as Pedn an Wlas and the Romans named the area Belerion, meaning seat of storms. A building calling itself the 'First and Last Refreshment House in England' is to be found here. Whether it's in England or not is debatable. Land's End is not actually a village but a point where the end of the land meets the sea and is sometimes referred to as 'the Land's End'. The famous privately owned mileage signpost here (est 1957) states that New York is 3,147 miles away, John O'Groats 874 miles, Longship Lighthouse 1.5 miles and the Isles of Scilly 28 miles away. Another part of this commercial tourist sign is left blank and for a fee can be personalised. The Cornish Way cycle and walking trail terminates here and it's where, on May 19th 2012, the London Olympics UK torch relay began. The initial torchbearer was Cornish born sailor and Olympic gold medallist, Ben Ainslie. Land's End Airport is situated on a private base at St Just (see 56).

The rugged beauty of Land's End cannot be denied although this iconic natural feature is somewhat overwhelmed by the popular commercial venture known as the Land's End Experience. Masses flock here to view this magnificent termination of land and sea, all needing to park, eat and be entertained. Admission to the Land's End site is free, although payment is required for parking and some attractions. If possible try to take time out to look beyond the man made and towards the spectacular natural environment, as its sheer beauty is stunningly overpowering.

On a clear day the Isles of Scilly (see 58) are visible. Nearby Sennen Cove is rather dominated by the lifeboat house and steep launch slope. The first and last pub in Cornwall is in Sennen, being very old, supposedly haunted and of course named the First and Last Inn. Ironically the pubs at the Lizard are actually further south. The area is a surfer's paradise and one of Europe's most popular body-boarding beaches. Look out for the book *The True Story of Bilbo the Surf Lifeguard Dog* (2008), which not only tells the story of an incredible Newfoundland dog but also gets across the important message of safety, such as always swimming between the red and yellow flags.

ISLES OF SCILLY

The Isles of Scilly (Enesek Syllan), sometimes known as the Paradise or Fortunate Isles, are an exotic, sub-tropical paradise situated about 28 miles from the Cornish mainland at Land's End and about 40 miles from Penzance. The region is considered separate to Cornwall and does in fact have its own flag and council, although the Duchy of Cornwall is custodian of most of the freehold land. Residents of the Isles of Scilly are referred to as Scillonians. There are hundreds of micro islets but the five main islands of the Scilly archipelago are St Mary's (Ennor), Tresco (Enys Skaw), St Martin's (Brechiek), Bryher (Breyer) and St Agnes (Aganas). It's thought that the Vikings knew the group of islands as Syllorgar and that they were also known as Sully (the sun islands). The white sandy beaches here are due to white quartz grains and milky feldspar granules resulting from granite erosion. Before rising sea levels flooded the former land, some of the islands were joined together as one large island, which the Romans knew as Ennor (Great Island). Such flooding may well have given rise to stories of the great lost kingdom of Lyonesse.

The rather isolated position of the Isles of Scilly (Syllan) from the rest of Cornwall (Kernow) gives it the feel of being continental and it's this very peripheral geography that makes it so special. The area enjoys an exceptionally mild, Oceanic, Gulf Stream climate, which is even warmer than mainland Cornwall and as a place where sub-tropical plants simply thrive it would be easy perhaps to compare the Isles of Scilly with the Italian Mediterranean island of Sicily (or even the Caribbean), as visually the sea and sand seem strikingly similar, right down to the palm trees! The sense of community here is palpable, life is tranquil and the pace of life is so relaxed it's worlds apart from the rat race of busy city life. From Penzance's south pier quay the sea ferry *Scillonian III* (launched 1977) travels to the Isles of Scilly (March-November) in under three hours. Short 'Skybus' flights to St Mary's airport can be taken from Land's End (15 min) and Newquay (30 min) airports. Sadly the helicopter service from Penzance closed in 2012, although there are plans for its return.

Apart from its wonderful climate, beauty and close proximity to mainland Cornwall, the Isles of Scilly are simply a superb 'paradise island' holiday destination. Boat trips, scenery, island hopping, pilot gig racing, archaeological wonders, tranquillity, glorious beaches, solitude, wildlife spotting (especially dolphins, seals, puffins and perhaps even choughs) and splendid walks are just a few of the things to enjoy, with the effort of getting here being well worth the simply breathtaking rewards. Even red squirrels travel to the Isles of Scilly as it's so idyllic, but be warned the weather and tidal conditions are crucial factors so always pay close attention to the state of the tide, especially when it's coming in, as there is a distinct danger of being cut off. If taking a boat trip make sure the return journey deadline isn't missed as strandings can happen! The Isles of Scilly are a designated Area of Outstanding Natural Beauty (AONB), a Conservation Area, has Heritage Coast status, is a Dark Night Sky Area and has over half its land mass designated Sites of Special Scientific Interest (SSSI).

St Mary's (in Cornish Ennor, meaning the mainland) is the hub island of the Isles of Scilly, the others being referred to as the off islands. It's the stepping-stone to the others and here is located the capital Hugh Town (Tre Huw), which derives its name from a geographical feature rather than from a person. The Hugh is a local peninsula, the name originating from *hoh* meaning a promontory or heel of land. Perched on top of it is the Elizabethan Star Castle (1593), now a luxury hotel complete with dungeon bar, which for Prince Charles (later King Charles II) afforded brief refuge in 1646 on his route to sanctuary in Jersey. The views are simply magnificent. The Penzance ferry ship docks at Hugh Town, with St Mary's Airport (est 1939) being located just outside (nearby) Old Town. A visit to the Island Museum in Church Street, Hugh Town, is a must, as are the numerous boat trips to the other islands and horse riding on sand and in the sea, with the riding centre located in Maypole close to Pelistry Beach. The Ales of Scilly Brewery (est 2001) 2B, Porthmellon, Hugh Town, makes for an interesting visit (view by appointment) The gardens of Carreg Dhu (free) near Holy Vale are worth viewing and bus and coach trips round the island are great fun. Halangy Down ancient Iron Age village and the nearby Bronze Age burial mound also makes for an interesting visit. Former Prime Minister and local resident Harold Wilson was buried on the island at St Mary's Old Church in 1995.

Tresco (Enys Skaw-island of elder trees) is a privately leased island and the location of the 17-acre Abbey Gardens (est 1834); also of interest there is the Valhalla Museum of ship figureheads. Shell collecting is a popular pastime and Piper's Hole at North End is a large and interesting cave to explore. Cromwell's Castle (1651) and King Charles' Castle (1550) nearer to New Grimsby are also worth visiting.

St Martin's island (Brechiek-dappled island) is home to the St Martin's Vineyard, Winery and Visitor Centre (est 1996) in Higher Town, where tours and wine sampling are certainly on the menu (check for opening).

Bryher (Breyer-place of hills) island is a place to enjoy nature's sheer beauty and at Shipman Head Down to wonder at the many prehistoric cairn (burial) mounds. Hell Bay is infamous for shipwrecks. The Bryher Fraggle Rock Bar is also well worth a visit.

St Agnes island (Aganas-off island) is known for its flower farming. The Turk's Head near Quay Slip (Britain's most westerly pub) at Porth Conger is highly recommended, as is visiting the Old Man of Gugh standing stone and Periglis beach. The pilot gig races are fun to watch and look out for tasty organic chocolate (flavoured with essential oils) from the Little Island Chocolate Company, which is made right here on St Agnes. At Beady Pool (Wingletang Bay) keep an eye open for small ceramic beads originating from an old 17th century Dutch shipwreck. Locals often refer to the island simply as Agnes.

South Cornwall

The relatively sheltered coast of South Cornwall stretches from Land's End right round to Cremyll on the Rame Peninsular. This is a distance of about 155 miles (250 km) or so and the wonderful Cornwall Coastal Path follows it round as it hugs the Cornish 'Riviera' coast, with the British Sea (English Channel) caressing its magnificent shoreline. The area is bursting with outstanding beauty and has countless treasures to share with those lucky enough to visit.

PORTHCURNO

In Cornish it's known as Porthkornow, importantly enough meaning port of Cornwall. Porthcurno has one main claim to fame that can be surmised from the name of the excellent, award winning, Telegraph Museum (est 1998) in Eastern House, as nearby is the stunning Porthcurno Beach, the site of the UK's first Trans-Atlantic underground telegraphy cables. The nearby Minack Open Air Theatre (est 1932) in Churchtown describes itself as 'Cornwall's Theatre Under the Stars'. It's an award winning real gem of a place being once voted the UK's best seaside attraction. In Cornish *minack* means a stony or rocky place and literally carved into the cliffs is this astonishing theatre, the brainchild of Rowena Cade (1893-1983). In the early days her home doubled up as a ticket office and the theatre was located at the end of her garden. The landscaped Minack Gardens are a delight in themselves and a sub-tropical treat not to be missed. Rowena's open-air theatre, with its appearance of a coastal Roman amphitheatre is an awe-inspiring memorial to an amazing woman.

Nearby is the Logan Rock, a large and heavy stone balanced precariously upon a more solid foundation. It was dislodged in 1824 by Lieutenant Hugh Goldsmith RN and a party of crewmen from HMS *Nimble*, who were duly ordered by the Admiralty to hoist it back on again. This they did although sadly it never rocked in quite the same way again and nowadays doesn't move at all. Legend has it that there is the occasional sighting of a ghost ship in the Porthcurno area that leaves the water and glides effortlessly over the ground!

At Lamorna Cove is a signpost on the Coastal Path leading to Oliver's Land Nature Reserve, which formed part of the Minack estate where Derek and Jeannie Tangye once lived and ran a flower farm. It was there that Derek wrote his *Minack Chronicles* series of over 20 books relating their exploits throughout years of their lives in the area. Just before his wife's death in 1986 Derek set up the Minack Chronicles Trust and donated the area for public use before his death in 1996. The Wink Inn in Lamorna is full of character and got its name from the time many years ago when those in the know winked to to the landlord for illicit spirits and some winked to local smugglers, turning a blind eye to their illegal pursuits, most probably in return for a share of the goods. At nearby St Buryan is the Neolithic Merry Maiden's stone circle consisting of 19 granite stones. Legend has it they were maidens turned to stone for disobeying strict church rules by dancing on a Sunday although they are actually much older than Christianity itself. By the side of the B3315 road and close to the Merry Maiden's site is the Neolithic Tregiffian Burial Chamber.

MOUSEHOLE

Mousehole has been described by some as the perfect Cornish harbour and more specifically by Dylan Thomas who lived here in 1930 as 'the loveliest village in England', although some would argue that England stops at the River Tamar. The name Mousehole is not pronounced 'mouse-hole' but 'mouzel', meaning uncertain in Cornish. It was formally known as Port Ennis and in Cornish is Porthenys meaning island cove, in reference to nearby St Clement's Isle. It's said that Mousehole might be named from the fact that the harbour was so hard and small to find it was like a mouse-hole but afforded safe shelter from the storm. Many small boats are tethered on long ropes in the harbour, giving the appearance of long-tailed mice all waiting to escape and rush through the gap in between the two arms of the concrete breakwaters. The lively working harbour is the focus of the whole village and clusters of character cottages encircle it. In 1595 the Spanish burned Mousehole to the ground leaving only one house intact. The lucky owner was Squire Keigwin although he died trying to extinguish the blaze. In later years his dwelling became a pub, the Keigwin Arms and a plaque outside the now privately owned building commemorates that fateful day, July 23rd 1595, when Keigwin died. Nearby is the house where Cornish speaker Dolly Pentreath once lived (see 3), being one of the last speakers of the Cornish language as her native tongue. She died in 1777 and is buried in nearby Paul village, where her large memorial stone can be seen set into the churchyard wall of St Paul Aurelian.

Every year in Mousehole, on the night before Christmas Eve, Star Gazy fish pies are consumed in memory of Tom Bawcock (see 28), with the Ship Inn at South Cliff at the centre of festivities. The walls of the pub are covered in old photographs, some of Tom Bawcock's Eve celebrations, others of the ill-fated crew of the Penlee lifeboat and a large one from 1967 showing the ill-fated wreck on Pollard's Rock of the oil super tanker *Torrey Canyon* which ran aground on 18th March 1967 on the Seven Stones Reef between the Isles of Scilly and Land's End as the captain tried to take a short cut to Milford Haven. The resulting pollution was an ecological disaster affecting over 100 miles of Cornish coastline. Admission to the Mousehole Wild Bird Hospital at Raginnis Hill is free (donations welcome); sisters Dorothy and Phyllis Yglesias first established the place in 1928 with the former writing two books about it, *The Cry of a Bird* in 1962 and *In Answer to the Cry* in 1978. In 1953 the RSPCA aided the Wild Bird Hospital but in 1975 they withdrew their support and it became an independent charity. The hospital's biggest challenge was helping thousands of affected birds during the *Torrey Canyon* oil disaster. Dorothy, Phyllis and the rest of the staff worked tirelessly to aid the stricken bird population and the sister's good work lives on.

In December 1981 disaster struck Mousehole when the local Penlee Point lifeboat *Solomon Browne* was lost with its crew of eight Mousehole men while going to the rescue of the coaster *Union Star*, which also sank and its crew of eight likewise drowned. There is now a memorial garden to commemorate the event and ever since the Mousehole Christmas harbour lights are switched off for an hour every December 19th as a mark of respect and remembrance for the gallant crews. The former lifeboat house is an empty shell standing like a giant headstone in memory of its brave lost occupants. The district lifeboat moved location in 1983 and is now housed at nearby Newlyn. Look out for the July bi-annual Sea, Salt & Sail Festival (est 1996) in celebration of Mousehole's marine heritage and traditions.

NEWLYN

Newlyn has been described as being as sweet as a rosebud. In Cornish it's known as Lulynn, meaning fleet pool, although some believe Newlyn to be named after the 5th century St Newlyna (St Newlina or St Nulyn). Newlyn is dominated by the fishing industry and a bronze statue has been erected on the beach in honour of the countless fishermen lost at sea. It has the UK's second largest fishing fleet and the massive harbour is over 40 acres in area. A plaque at the old quay celebrates the fact that in 1620 the Pilgrim Fathers' ship *Mayflower* briefly anchored there to take on water and supplies before setting sail on its journey to America. In 1851 84-year-old Newlyn fishwife Mary Kelynack walked 300 miles to London to attend the Crystal Palace Great Exhibition. She wore her traditional fish cowl clothing and wanted to bring attention to the problems of the Cornish fishing industry. It took Mary five weeks to complete her task and she not only arrived safely but was even lucky enough to meet Queen Victoria.

In 1854 seven Cornishmen decided, over a few pints at the Star Hotel (now the Star Inn) on The Strand, to journey to Australia and try their luck prospecting for gold. It was a 116 day, 12,000-mile trip, from Newlyn to Melbourne in an open 37ft Mounts Bay Lugger named *Mystery* (PE 233). Happily they found the gold they strived for but not exactly in the quantities they desired. There is a plaque commemorating this extraordinary adventure on the wall of the Newlyn Royal Mission to Seamen at the Ship Institute, North

Pier. Pete Goss bravely recreated this epic journey with some of his friends in his replica Cornish Lugger *Spirit of Mystery*. He achieved success on the 9th March 2009, with the journey taking five months to complete. In 1896 there were riots when non-Cornish 'foreign' fishermen from Lowestoft and other northern ports converged on Newlyn in order to land and sell their fish on a Sunday, thus breaking the tradition of not working on the Sabbath. Soldiers and a naval destroyer were eventually deployed to restore order and the outsiders were soon sent packing.

Newlyn boasts the world's only working Cornish fishing lugger, named the *Ripple* (built in 1896) but is best known for another vessel. In 1937 local fishing boat *Rosebud* (Lugger PZ 87) sailed to London in protest against proposed slum clearances in Newlyn; residents were to be moved from their old homes in the heart of the village community, into new homes well away from the harbour. They all had connections with the fishing industry in some form or other and felt their heritage was being threatened. The angry crew delivered a petition to the government at Westminster and some homes were actually saved. In memory of this heroic journey a plaque was placed on the Newlyn Mission and the Rosebud Memorial Garden was established in the St Peter's Hill area where much of the clearances took place. Ironically the demolition site is now a conservation area. Eventually *Rosebud* fell into disrepair and rotted away. A quantity of her wood was salvaged by locals and became treasured mementoes, some even being carved into miniature models of the boat itself. The story is a fascinating one of Cornish fishermen fighting for what was rightfully theirs against the powers that be and their quest has gone down in the annals of history.

The Newlyn School of Art was a rival to St Ives, first established in the 1880s by Stanhope Forbes and Walter Langley. They painted outdoor scenes of village life dominated by fishermen at work. Many examples of their paintings and others are displayed at the Penlee House Gallery & Museum in Penlee Park, just off Alverton Road. The Newlyn Pilchard Works at Tolcarne was the only working salt pilchard factory left in Britain but is now just another modern conversion into apartments. By the lighthouse at the end of the south pier is an unassuming collection of buildings and it was here that the Ordnance Survey calculated basic sea level between 1915 and 1921. It's known as the Ordnance Datum (ODN) point and all other heights throughout Great Britain are calculated using this Newlyn measure of sea level. Political radical and reformist William Lovett (1800-1877) was born in Newlyn and became leader of the Chartist Movement.

PENZANCE

Penzance means holy headland from the Cornish name Pennsans, with *pen* meaning headland and *sans* meaning holy. It's been described as the capital of west Cornwall. In 1663 King Charles II declared Penzance a new coinage town for the tin industry. Maria Branwell, mother to the Bronte sisters, was born locally in 1783 and her house at 25, Chapel Street, displays a stone plaque to celebrate the fact. For many, Penzance brings to mind Gilbert and Sullivan's operetta *The Pirates of Penzance*, first performed in London in 1880. In Alverton there's even a pub called the Pirate Inn Penzance!

Sir Humphry Davy was born in Penzance in 1778 and a statue of him stands proudly outside the old town hall in Market Street. Pigeons have adopted his statue as an obligatory resting place and his nearby house is now a shop. Sir Humphry discovered laughing gas (nitrous oxide), chlorine, iodine, sodium, potassium, calcium and in 1815 invented the Davy Lamp, a revolutionary safety lamp that didn't cause explosions in mines. He died in 1829 and his statue is worthy tribute to a great Cornishman. Opposite is the Tremenheere Wetherspoon's pub; its name derives from the surname of ten mayors of Penzance, uncommonly all descendants of the same family, from the first in 1655 to the final one in 1797. Down the road on Sir Humphry's side look out for the quaint curved granite steps leading up from the road to the shop level terrace.

Penzance enjoys an annual June celebration known as the Golowan Festival, which harks back to ancient midsummer rituals and fire festivals, with fireworks, greenery and community events. The festivities reach their peak on Mazey Day when a burning torch procession, a hobby-horse known as Penglaz, the Serpent Dance and such make their way through the local streets. The festival fell out of favour for many years as it was banned in the 1890s but was revived again in 1991 and has thrived ever since. The Crown pub, located in Victoria Square is partly supplied by its own microbrewery at Gulval, aptly named the Cornish Crown Brewery. At nearby Crowlas is the Star Inn, home to the Penzance Brewing Company (est 2008). The Admiral Benbow in Chapel Street is a 17th century smuggler's pub complete with a secret tunnel, Cornish flags and a model of a mutineer pirate or possibly of Admiral John Benbow (1653-1702) himself, perched on the roof in full period dress with gun in hand. It has also been mooted that the model depicts the story of a young volunteer who climbed up onto the roof to shoot at a nearby chimney in order to distract the revenue men who were planning to raid the premises. Sadly he was shot, fell off the roof but survived to become a local hero. Also in Chapel Street is the historic 17th century Union Hotel with its rare c1786 theatre building (closed in 1831). It was in the hotel's Georgian dining room, formally Penzance's original public assembly room (est 1791), that the victory at the Battle of Trafalgar and the death of Admiral Horatio Nelson was first publicly announced in Britain, due to local fishermen intercepting a ship bound for Falmouth bearing news of the event. In 1595 Spanish raiders destroyed most of the original building and some of the stonework in the main bar is testament to this. The Union Hotel building first became a hotel in 1825.

The unique Egyptian House in Chapel Street was built in 1836 as a geological museum and is now owned and managed by the Landmark Trust, occasionally open to the public. The Cornish Pirates rugby union team, previously known as the Penzance Pirates, are currently based at the Mennaye Field ground at Westholme, Alexandra Road. In 1987 Ginni Little established the Cornwall Bat Hospital in Alma Terrace to rehabilitate sick and injured bats and then return them to the wild. The three-acre Morrab Garden (free entry) is a haven of tranquillity within Penzance, located off St Mary's Terrace. Within the grounds is the independent Morrab Library (est 1818). Its land was once seashore which in Cornish is *mor ap,* hence the name. Penlee House Gallery & Museum in Morrab Road is also worth a visit; in the grounds is a medieval granite cross to King Ricatus of Cornwall. Dating from around 1050, it's inscribed *Regis Ricati Crux* (Cross of King Ricatus) and once stood in Penzance's Greenmarket as the market cross.

The old Dolphin Tavern in Quay Street is allegedly haunted by at least one of the unfortunate men who fell foul of the infamous 'Hanging Judge Jeffries', who held sessions there in what is now the dining room, in the mid 1700s. Barrels of hidden brandy have apparently been discovered here in modern times and there's talk of a ghostly sea captain haunting the building. In 1585 the tavern was used as a base to recruit sailors for the Armada and it also has connections with Sir Walter Raleigh (1552-1618) as it's thought to be the first place a pipe of tobacco was smoked in this country. Penzance's promenade is usually festooned with a series of colourful flags and the popular outdoor Jubilee Pool seaside lido is located here in Battery Road. This stylish, triangular art deco pool was designed by Captain F. Latham, opened in 1935 and is now a listed structure. It's the largest tidal sea water, open-air swimming pool still in use in the United Kingdom.

From Penzance quay the *Scillonian III* sea ferry can be boarded to visit the Isles of Scilly, which are a popular holiday destination (see 58). Although the helicopter service to the islands ceased operations in 2012, there are plans for its possible return. On a large granite stone outside Penzance railway station in Wharf Road is proudly carved 'PENSANS A'GAS DYNERGH - PENZANCE WELCOMES YOU'. The station was opened in 1852 by the West Cornwall Railway and is the most western station in Cornwall and the terminus for the Cornish Riviera Express out of Paddington station, London. A local railway service from Penzance to St Ives is the St Ives Bay line and along its scenic miles of track a Real Ale Trail has been set up; passengers have full use of that part of the railway and can stop off at stations whenever they wish. Just outside Penzance, at nearby Madron, is Trengwainton Garden and also the ancient Madron Well (or St Madron's Well), a sacred site where strips of cloth known as clouties are ritually tied to nearby trees. This site of pilgrimage has been popular for many centuries and has a strange, atmospheric feel to it. Near Madron is the Men an Tol (Men-an-Toll) ancient standing stones site, the name literally meaning stone and hole in Cornish. There are many legends attached to this famous 'rock doughnut' megalith, especially concerning the healing powers of the middle circular stone, with its carved hole that's large enough for a child or small adult to pass through. It's an iconic place to visit, as is close by Lanyon Quoit, another most impressive Neolithic ancient monument. Newmill is the location of Chysauster Ancient Village, the remains of an almost 2,000-year-old Iron Age settlement (restricted opening times). Tremenheere Sculpture Gardens (1997) are located between Gulval and Ludgvan.

MARAZION

Marazion apparently enjoys the most temperate climate of mainland Britain and on average has more sunshine than anywhere else. The town's name rhymes with iron, is pronounced rather like 'marry-zion' and is known as the gateway to St Michael's Mount. It claims to be one of the oldest towns in Britain and is known in Cornish as Marhasyow, meaning Thursday Market. The Romans knew it as Ictis but Marazion may simply mean small sea, referring to the narrow stretch of water between the village and St Michael's Mount. Charles II is said to have stayed in a nearby house in 1646 as he was escaping to the Isles of Scilly after the Royalist defeated at Naseby.

Five thousand year old fossil tree stumps and roots can be found at very low tides and even underwater six miles from shore. In Cornish the name for the mount, Karrek Loos yn Koos, means hoar rock in the wood, with hoar meaning greyish-white in colour and the rock in question being granite. According to the Saxon Chronicles Lyonesse, the now legendary lost land, was obliterated in 1099 whilst others say in 1089 or even earlier around the 6th century. Whenever it was, the land and towns were flooded with apparently all human and animal life drowned. It's said that ghostly bells from that ancient land can occasionally still be heard above the crashing of Cornish waves. The Godolphin Arms Hotel at Marazion's West End derives its unusual name from the Godolphin family who made their fortune from the mining industry and lived in Godolphin House, their fifteenth century manor near Helston.

The St Aubyn family on St Michael's Mount have a 17th century marriage connection with the Godolphin's. The pub is in the ownership of the St Aubyn family and weddings are often conducted in the main room. The views over to St Michael's Mount from the Godolphin Arms Hotel are unrestricted and the walkway over to the Mount is directly below the pub.

St Michael's Mount has been described as the jewel in Cornwall's crown. The priory was built in 1135 under orders from the Benedictine Abbot Bernard of Normandy's Mont St Michel, hence the similarity. This island of history is now National Trust owned (since 1954) and has been home since 1659 to the St Aubyn family, who are still in residence. The medieval castle can be reached by walking over there at low tide. At other times a ferry journey is required. If crossing, take note of the state of the tide, always err on the side of caution and thus avoid risk. Legend has it that a wicked giant named Cormoran built St Michael's Mount and made his home there. He stole cattle from the mainland and so the locals called for an end to it all and especially to him. Eventually a boy named Jack came forward with a plan. He dug a huge hole and blew a horn to summon Cormoran at dawn. The sleepy giant tried to catch him but because the sun was in his eyes he failed to see the hole and fell down it. Quickly Cormoran was buried and died, so Jack the 'giant killer' became a hero and everyone lived happily ever after. Look out for Cormoran's stone heart neatly placed amongst the cobblestone pathway on the way up to the castle. It's said if you stand on it you can hear the giant's heartbeat and its diminutive size is due to the fact that he had little love for anyone or anything.

In 1497 Perkin Warbeck left his wife, the Lady Catherine, safely tucked up in bed on the Mount and went off to make his ill-fated attempt on the English crown of King Henry VII and was eventually executed for his efforts in 1499. In 1588 the Spanish Armada was sighted from the Mount and sanctuary was apparently given in 1642-1643 to King Charles II, whilst on his way to safety in the Isles of Scilly; the Royalist's surrendered the Mount in 1646 to the attacking Parliamentarians. The Mount's 20-acre terraced garden is well worth viewing but castle and gardens are closed on Saturdays. The Mount has its own harbour and small village community. It's free to walk over and look around the harbour area, with its shops and café and there's always the option of a ferry across if the state of the tide decrees it. Look out for a foot-shaped brass plate on the floor of the landing stage, commemorating Queen Victoria's first step onto the island in 1846. Both Queen Elizabeth II and the Duke of Edinburgh left permanent casts of their footprints at the base of the castle when they visited the island in 2013. There is no pub on St Michael's Mount nowadays but there used to be three, including the Jolly Tinner and the John Tyack. The last one to survive was the St Aubrey Arms, which closed in 1902.

The Marazion museum in the Market Place is worth a visit, as is the nearby RSPB reserve at Marazion Marsh where flocks of starlings form a magnificent spectacle whenever they roost there, often flying in an impressive acrobatic formation known as a murmuration. This protected area was designated a Site of Special Scientific Interest (SSSI) back in 1951. According to legend a ghostly apparition of a lady in white is occasionally sighted in Marazion around the area of the Green, where she climbs onto the back of a horse before being whisked away by the rider, just as she did apparently in 1471. In Victorian times Marazion was also well known for a delicious species of… turnip! Nearby is Pengersick Castle, located in Pengersick Lane at Praa (pronounced 'pray') Sands, which was rebuilt about 1530 as a fortified Tudor manor. It's reputed to be the most haunted building in Britain and its medieval grounds form part of a garden trail. At nearby Rosehill is the Polgoon Vineyard and Cider Orchard (est 2006), which specialises in producing Cornish wines and ciders.

PORTHLEVEN

Porthleven has been described as a Cornish Treasure and lies at the heart of Bath Oliver Country. It has the distinction of being mainland Britain's most southerly port. In Cornish Porthleven is spelt the same, meaning the port of St Elvan, although as *leven* means smooth in Cornish the name might be derived from smooth port or cove. The inventor of Bath Oliver biscuits, Dr William Oliver (1695-1764), was born close by at Sithney. Wing Commander Guy Penrose Gibson (1918-1944), best known for his heroic World War II role as first commanding officer in charge of the RAF's 617 Dam Busters Squadron, lived here as a child from the age of three. He was awarded a Victoria Cross in 1943 for his efforts and is held in proud esteem by the village. Helston born cabinet maker Henry Trengrouse (1772-1854) witnessed a shipwreck at nearby Loe Bar in 1807 and this inspired him to invent his rocket line rescue apparatus that is still in use today. Its ship to shore chair and pulley system has saved countless lives over the years and is now simply known as Breeches Buoy rather than Trengrouse's Lifeline. Rick Stein's harbourside restaurant is in Mount Pleasant Road.

Up on the hill by the harbour entrance is a cross in memory of the many sailors who were drowned and buried in the vicinity. It also commemorates the Grylls' Act of 1808 which allowed bodies washed ashore to be buried in the nearest consecrated ground rather than just buried on the cliff top in unconsecrated ground as before if their religion was unknown. The act was named after its instigator, local solicitor Thomas Grylls. In 1912 a great storm in the cove shifted some of the beach sand and exposed a large number of Spanish pieces of eight silver coins. On the beach below Rinsey Cliff at Porthcew there is an interesting geological feature where contact between granite and slate can be clearly seen and also a giant rock consisting of garnet and gneiss. Nearby Prussia Cove was once the land of the Carter Family who were notorious smugglers. John Carter (1738-1803) was known as the 'King of Prussia' and based himself on Frederick the Great of Prussia, hence the nickname. Prussia Cove was originally called Porthleah but John Carter's influence resulted in it being renamed. His brothers assisted in keeping the smuggling business a homely, family affair although Harry Carter (1749-1829) eventually saw the error of his ways, became a Methodist preacher and even wrote a book about his wayward and subsequently transformed life.

Nearby is Goonhilly Satellite Earth Station. The huge white saucers look surreal even for planet Earth, never mind rural Cornwall. Goonhilly means hunting pasture, being derived from the Cornish word *goon*, a hilly area of down land and *helgh* meaning hunting. It was here in 1962 that the first flickering transatlantic television pictures were received from America via Telstar on satellite dish Antenna One which is nicknamed Arthur after... King Arthur. The other dishes are likewise named Guinevere, Merlin etc. The dishes are no longer in use and the site, once a huge tourist attraction, is presently closed to the public but has been recently developed by Goonhilly Earth Station (GES) Ltd as a commercial deep space network communications and radio-astronomy research facility. A Space Science Park is planned along with a re-vamped visitor centre. In the meantime co-ordination skills can be tried out on an electric, self-balancing 'scooter' transporter at the Cornwall Segway centre there. Poldhu Cove is overlooked by the old Poldhu Hotel (c1899), which has the appearance of a grand Victorian castle but is now in fact a nursing home. Guglielmo Marconi set up a wireless telegraphy station at the top of the cliffs and it was here on December 12th 1901 that the first transatlantic signals were sent and received from Canada. In his honour, the Poldhu Amateur Radio Club opened the Marconi Centre (2001) which has exhibits and information about Marconi, built in the field where he sent his historic signal. The centre was opened 100 years to the day of the first signal being sent: the letter 'S' was sent and 'R' was the reply. The nearby Marconi monument was built in 1937.

The Loe or Loe Pool is Cornwall's largest natural freshwater lake. It's also claimed to be where Excalibur was thrown into and that every seven years the pool claims a life. The pool actually formed because the River Caber flows into it but Loe Bar blocks its way to the sea. In legend, Jan Tregeagle (or Tregagle) was so bad that he sold his soul to the Devil. He was then summoned back to this world as a witness in a court case but instead of returning to Hell he was forced for eternity to complete the impossible task of emptying all the water out of Bodmin Moor's Dozmary Pool using only a limpet shell with a hole in it. After years at the task he managed to escape, only to be stuck in the window of Roche Rock hermitage. His howls could be heard for miles before he was released and forced for ever to weave ropes from sand down at Gwenor Cove. Once he spilt a sack of sand near Porthleven and that, so they say, was how Loe Bar was formed. The Tregeagle legend is actually based upon a real person, one John Tregeagle (or Tregagle) who was a 17th century Justice of the Peace and squire of Trevorder in St Breoke, near Truro. He acquired land by both fair and foul means, was a harsh landlord and was even rumoured to have murdered his wife. He died in 1655 and the legend developed around his despised memory. When Cornish storms blow furiously it's said that Tregeagle's voice is often still heard howling relentlessly along with them, even down peoples chimneys and crying children were likened to having Tregeagle's roar. Gold coins are sometimes found around the coast here, originating from Dutch and Spanish wrecks. Another treasure is the rare Cornish Rustic Sandhill Moth, first discovered around the shingle of Loe Bar in 1974. It's a pale brownish colour and unique to the area but is sadly in grave danger of extinction as only a small colony still survives.

HELSTON

The ancient stannary town of Helston is known as the gateway to the Lizard peninsular and in Cornish is referred to as Hellys meaning old court, in reference to the tin miner's old Stannary Court held here as part of the legal branch of the Stannary Parliament. Helston is best known for its May Day celebrations but locally born boxer Bob Fitzsimmons (1863-1917) made history by being the first world champion boxer in three divisions: middleweight, light heavyweight and heavyweight. Bob was also the first boxer to be recorded on film. Coinagehall Street is so called because tin was once assessed for payable tax here, a procedure referred to as the tin being coined.

The 15th century Blue Anchor Inn is located at 50 Coinagehall Street and the owners even run a B&B next door. Not only does the pub have its own microbrewery, which is open to the public upon request but it also boasts a skittle alley, its own supply of fresh spring water, a huge granite inglenook fireplace and welcomes well behaved dogs. It's affectionately known as the Blue and the master brewer, Tim Sears, wrote the *The Blue Anchor, Helston, The First 600 Years* (2002) about it, a fascinating insight into the history of the pub and its brewing. The new Wetherspoon's pub, the Coinage Hall, is located at 9-11 Coinage Street. The Helston Folk Museum in Market Street was established in 1949 and entry is free, although donations are welcome. Running through Helston is a quaint old system of narrow granite kerbside water channels, known as kennels. Before the days of indoor plumbing these conduits supplied a source of fresh water from the local River Cober to the townsfolk and their various business enterprises. The ornate patterns in the surrounding paving stones are functional as well as decorative, providing a non-slip surface for pedestrians as well as surface water run off channels. Water pumps were a local source of drinking water and perhaps the kennels were used for this purpose.

The May Day celebrations in Helston were originally in honour of the pre-Christian festival of the passing of winter and the coming of spring. Many traditional festivities are enjoyed on the actual day and a large brass band tours the town playing the Floral Dance tune. This should strictly be called the Furry Dance because the day was originally called Furry Day, possibly deriving from the Cornish word *fuer* meaning either fair or holiday. It's also referred to as Flora Day, with Flora being the goddess of flowers and of spring. Floral is a corruption of Flora and just describes the flower part of the meaning. Look out for traditional Helston Pudding (Podin Henlys), especially on Flora/Furry Day, as it's a delicious steamed pudding rather like a light-textured Christmas pudding but with the addition of rice flour. Nowadays Helston's Furry Dance is associated with the *Floral Dance* song that was actually written in 1911 by Katie Moss, although a small part was apparently gleaned from an old Cornish melody.

The ceremony of Beating the Bounds is performed annually to mark the ancient parish boundaries of the town. Strangely enough though, they don't use sticks to beat the granite boundary stones with but volunteers' heads, cushioned with a local turf of grass! The nearby Gweek National Seal Sanctuary at the head of the Helford river has been rescuing, rehabilitating and releasing seals for over 50 years. It started back in 1958 when Ken Jones discovered a young seal pup stranded on the beach at St Agnes. In 1975 his rescue site there was too small and so the Gweek centre was established. It's now Europe's busiest seal rescue centre and is open to the public every day apart from Christmas Day. It's also a rescue centre for sea lions, otters, goats and ponies and the entrance fee pays towards their upkeep. In Cornish Gweek is known as Gwyk with *wyk* meaning creek. It was once a thriving port and tin was brought here from Helston to be shipped out all over the world. Charles Kingsley, author of *The Water-Babies* (1863), attended nearby Helston Grammar School.

Just outside Helston is Royal Naval Air Station (RNAS) Culdrose, commissioned as HMS *Seahawk*. At Culdrose Manor is Flambards Theme Park (est 1976) and near Helston is the impressive 15th century Godolphin House located at Godolphin Cross. At Poldark Mine & Museum at nearby Wendron a genuine 18th century tin mine can be viewed, while at Rosuick Organic Farm in nearby St Martin camels can be found. Yes camels! Booking in advance is essential.

MULLION

Mullion (formally Mullyon) is named after the 6th century St Melaine. In Cornish the village is known as Eglosvelyan, meaning church of St Melan and is the largest village on the Lizard Peninsular. Legend has it that some of the pasties in these parts are a big as rugby balls. About three miles away is the beautiful Mullion harbour, which is well worth seeing. Mullion Island is said to take on the appearance of a crouching lion at around mid-tide. In Cornish the island is called Enys Pryven, meaning island of snakes. Nearby Kynance Cove is named after the Cornish word *kewnans*, meaning ravine and *ky* means dog in Cornish. It has a profusion of serpentine and the caves have wonderful names such as the Devil's Mouth and the Devil's Letter Box. Bishop's Rock even looks like it has a face on it. Located not far from Mullion is the small village of... Cury! It was formally known as Corantyn and in Cornish is Egloskun (formally Egoskuri). It's named after St Corentin(e), a 5th century French saint of Brittany, anciently referred to as St Chori. Located within the parish of Cury on the A3083 road at Cury Cross Lanes is the Wheel Inn, where you can have a curry in Cury, akin to having sweets in Sweets (a village near Crackington Haven), or going to the loo in Looe!

LIZARD

The Lizard Peninsula is the most southerly part of mainland UK and in Cornish is known as Lysardh, with *lys* meaning court or palace and *ardh* meaning high, although perhaps derived from the old word lazar meaning leper. The nearby church of St Wynwallows in Landewednack, which in Cornish is known as Lanndewynnek, meaning the church site of St Winwalo, was possibly the last in old Cornwall where a sermon was preached in Cornish in 1678. Lizard village (or Lizard Green) was once known as Lizard Town and on first appearance seems nowadays to consist solely of a grassy car park surrounded on three sides by gift shops with distant views of the sea to the fourth. A visit to Ann's Pasties in Beacon Terrace is almost obligatory when visiting the area, just look out for the yellow house! A walk down to Church Cove is certainly a must and some lucky visitors even get to see the Cornish heath heather, which is so rare it's only found on the Lizard Peninsular. It's considered by many to be the flower of Cornwall and between July and September its pink and white flowers cover the heathland. Another rarity is the Lizard juniper of which there were only 13 known wild specimens recorded in 2013, although the Eden Project runs a conservation programme aimed at saving the species from extinction.

The Lizard Peninsular contains Pre-Cambrian metamorphic rocks that are an estimated 640 million years old and are the oldest rocks in Cornwall. Around the Lizard serpentine is found in abundance and its carving is a local cottage industry. Queen Victoria and Prince Albert initiated this interest in 1846 when they visited these parts as they thought the rock so unusual and interesting. Locals have been mining and shaping it ever since. Serpentine isn't just green, impurities can cause it to be shades of red or black and it often has a mottled appearance with white or red veins running through it. Its name derives from its similarity to snake skin and carved serpentine ornaments are very popular. The Lizard Ales Brewery is located on the disused radar station site of nearby RAF Treleaver and the Cornish Chough Brewery at Trethvas Farm. Nearby Cadgwith Cove is well worth visiting; in Cornish it's known as Porth Kajwydh, meaning cove of the thicket.

COVERACK

In Cornish Coverack is known as Porthkovrek meaning hideaway or hidden place. Coverack can be described as a place where crust meets mantle, as here a geological rarity is exposed for the entire world to see. The junction between the Earth's crust and the deeper layers of Earth's mantle lie uncovered on the shore. The mantle area and pieces of it have been incorporated into the harbour breakwater itself. They are very dark in colour, dense in appearance, deeply cracked and look and are incredibly ancient. Looking out to sea from the road, the crustal rocks to the left of the shore (north) are made of gabbro and to the right of the shore (south) are the darker, once deeper mantle peridodite rocks containing serpentine. At the other end of the bay the crustal rocks feature. Somewhere in between, among the houses and the sea, they meet. The junction between these two layers was named after its discoverer, Croatian seismologist Andrija Mohorovicic, in 1909. As his name is so difficult to pronounce it was shortened and the feature is universally known as the Moho for short and the Mohorovicic Discontinuity for long. By the car park on the outskirts of the village a most helpful information board clearly explains the complex geology of Coverack.

The old lifeboat station here has been converted to the Lifeboat House Restaurant, complete with ex-RNLI launch ramp. This, together with the Paris Hotel, dominates the harbour area, as does an honesty-box car park and four lifeboat boards detailing rescues from 1902-1978. The Paris Hotel was named after the SS *Paris*, an American passenger liner that ran aground in 1899 off Lowland Point, part of the deadly Manacles Reef. Miraculously nobody was killed then but other ships and their crews have not been so lucky. Every Christmas Day the annual Coverack charity swim takes place and the participants dress up in all sorts of weird and wonderful attire. Coverack has given its name to at least three types of daffodil, namely Coverack Glory, Coverack Beauty and Coverack Perfection. The Harbour Lights beach café is worth frequenting. Near to Coverack is Roskilly's Ice Cream Organic Farm at Tregellast Barton, St Keverne; it's free to visit and the ice cream is a delight. Look out for it on sale locally.

HELFORD

Helford has been described as the gateway to Cornwall's most unspoilt river. Its name derives from the fact that it's positioned on the bank of the River Helford at a shallow crossing point. In Cornish it's known as simply Heyl or Heylfordh, with *heyl* meaning estuary. Boat trips and the Helford Ferry are great ways to experience the River Helford. One inlet has literary connections as Frenchman's Creek was made famous by a book of the same name, written by Daphne du Maurier (1907-1989) in 1941. She honeymooned in the area in 1932 and was inspired to write a pirate love story. At nearby Mawnan Smith can be found the Trebah and Glendurgan Gardens.

FALMOUTH

Falmouth has been rightly described as the heart of maritime Cornwall and its name derives from its position on the mouth of the River Fal. The popularity of Falmouth is evident from the fact that it was voted by the *Sunday Times* as the fourth best place to live in Britain (2014). In Cornish Falmouth is known as Aberfala, with *aber* meaning river mouth or meeting of waters. It was formally known as Smithwick (or Smithick) and later as Peny-cym-cuic, which slipped into the obvious slang name of Penny-come-quick, an early reference perhaps to its increasing commercial popularity. There are some good beaches in Falmouth, namely Castle beach, Tunnel beach, Gyllyngvase beach, Swanpool beach, and a little further out but well worth the trip, is Maenporth beach. The area by the main bus station is known as Falmouth Moor and the Wetherspoon's pub there, The Packet Station (est 2003), is named in honour of the overseas postal (packet) system established at Falmouth in 1688. There is a Packet Service memorial obelisk at the Moor in celebration of this cherished Post Office heritage.

A rather ominous flight of granite steps is located in the Moor area and is known locally as 'Jacob's Ladder'. It consists of 111 steps in total, although some say it's 112. They were constructed in the 1840s by Jacob Hamblen who used them daily in connection with his business at the bottom and his property interests at the top. The Jacob's Ladder Inn at the summit is a welcome sight indeed for thirsty travellers. The Falmouth Art Gallery (free) is housed in the Municipal Buildings on the Moor and was established in 1978. Robert Were Fox (1789-1877) was a local man and in 1822 discovered that the temperature of the Earth actually increases the deeper one goes into the core; in the 1830s he developed the dip circle needle compass for use at sea. Another local was author W.J. Burley (1914-2002) and from his many *Wycliffe* detective novels the 1990s television series was created, starring Jack Shepherd as DC Charles Wycliffe.

In the old harbour area is a furnace and chimney known locally as the King's Pipe, where any smuggled tobacco captured by the customs men was destroyed for all to see. The Front Bar at Custom House Quay is highly recommended, as is Rick Stein's Fish & Seafood Restaurant at Discovery Quay and the award winning National Maritime Museum of Cornwall (2003), which is certainly worth a lengthy visit. Opposite the National Maritime Museum is a rather large, tall, granite obelisk, built in 1737 in memory of Martin Lister Killigrew and his wife's family. Mr Killigrew's wife had aristocratic ancestors who founded Falmouth in around 1613. Nearby Arwenack House in Grove Place, the oldest building in Falmouth, was the Killigrew family seat and has its origins in 1385. It was rebuilt in 1567, destroyed by fire in 1646 and has since been rebuilt frequently and influenced by many styles. For all their wealth and standing, one of the family rather let the side down, as Lady Mary Killigrew (1530-1570) was a notorious pirate, murderess and thief!

Falmouth has the distinction of being the third largest natural deep-water harbour in the world. The Fal is a large ria, meaning it's a large flooded post-glacial valley and there is a story that a giant sea creature named Morgawr has been sighted out in the bay, presumably living somewhere in the vicinity in the murky depths below. Falmouth has a great sea-faring tradition going back centuries and more recently Robin Knox-Johnston became the first man to circumnavigate the globe sailing non-stop and single-handed, having started from here on the 14th June 1968 and returned on the 22nd April 1969. For many years the famous tea clipper *Cutty Sark* was moored in Falmouth harbour. Pendennis Worldclass

Superyachts are hand built here and the company produces top of the range yachts, some costing millions of pounds to purchase. The International Sea Shanty Festival is held annually at the same time as the Falmouth Classics Regatta.

Pendennis Castle, which was built almost five hundred years ago by order of Henry VIII in order to keep out French and Spanish invaders, is worth a visit. A special railway journey from Falmouth to Truro is known as the Maritime Line and along its scenic miles of track a Real Ale Trail has been set up. For the cost of a ticket passengers have full use of that part of the railway for the day and can get on and off the train at will. Fans of Brad Pitt will be interested to learn that parts of the zombie thriller film *World War Z* (2011) were filmed in the Falmouth area.

TRURO

In modern Cornish Truro is known as Truru. The name might well be derived from the Cornish *tri veru* meaning three rivers, in this case the Allen, Tinney and Kenwyn, which converge to form the Truro River. It may be named from the Cornish *tri berow*, which describes the three (fast flowing) rivers as turbulent or boiling. Some dispute these explanations believing the name to come from the Cornish *tru ru* meaning castle on the water, although the castle has long since disappeared. Nowadays the city is often referred to as 'proud Truro', with its residents being known as Truronians. It's situated more or less in the centre of Cornwall, was once a stannary town and only became a city in 1877. It's Cornwall's administrative capital and its magnificent cathedral is Truro's jewel in the crown. Although it may appear old and steeped in history, it's actually rather modern, being built between 1880-1910 on the site of St Mary's church. Edward White Benson (1829-1896) was the first Bishop of Truro (1877-1882) and in 1880 he introduced the first ever Festival of Nine Lessons and Carols, which is now celebrated internationally every Christmas. The cathedral is one of only three in the UK boasting three spires!

The Royal Cornwall Museum (est 1818) in River Street is the largest and oldest museum in Cornwall. Although there is no admission fee, a charge may be made for special exhibitions. Skinners Brewery was founded in Truro in 1997 at Riverside, Newham Road and is a great attraction to lovers of real ale. Like the St Austell Brewery, it runs regular brewery tours and gives visitors the opportunity to sample the beer. Despite being so far inland, Truro is actually a port located at the head of the Fal Estuary. Lemon Quay sounds as though its name is derived from imported cargoes of citrus fruit but in fact it refers to Sir Richard Lemon who developed the area. Lemon Street is also named in his honour and the Try Dowr Wetherspoon's pub here, established in 2006, has opted to call itself after the alternate spelling of the *tri veru* three rivers derivation of Truro's name. The Lemon Quay piazza area close to the cathedral is a vibrant part of the city, with markets and events taking place throughout the year. Tim Shaw's controversial statue of a naked, male drummer is on view here, apparently symbolising Cornwall as a place where the drum beats differently. It was unveiled in 2011 by Queen drummer Roger Taylor. The Lander Memorial in Lemon Street was erected in 1835 in honour of two local brothers, Richard and John Lander, who discovered the source of the River Niger in 1827. The Truro to Falmouth Real Ale Trail has been established on the Maritime Line (see 70). Truro Boscawen Park and the gardens of Trellissick and Bosvigo near Truro are of great horticultural interest.

ST MAWES

This is a truly a beautiful, bustling place with a distinct, almost French feel about it. The name is derived from the 5th/6th century Celtic Saint Maudez (St Mawe) and a holy well dedicated to him still exists at Victory Hill, close to the Victory Inn. In Cornish St Mawes is known as Lannvowsedh, possibly meaning an enclosed holy seat. St Mawes Castle located on Castle Drive is 16th century and, like Falmouth's Pendennis Castle, was built under instruction from Henry VIII. Both castles were completed between 1539 and

1545. St Mawes castle has three large circular towers (or bastions) built in a three-leaf clover design. It's panoramic harbour views that are breathtaking. Barry Bucknell, keen yachtsman and television DIY presenter from the 1950s and early 60s, called this area home until his death in 2003. In 1962 along with a colleague he designed the highly popular 'Mirror class' dinghy. Hotel Tresanton is owned and run by interior designer Olga Polizzi, sister of Sir Rocco Forte. The Idle Rocks (est 1913) is a luxury hotel right by the beach and a cream tea on their balcony overlooking the splendid harbour is an amazing experience. A short ferry ride away is the three and a half mile Roseland Ramble complete with lighthouse experience. Not far from St Mawes is the small scenic fishing village of Portscatho, which makes for an interesting visit. In Cornish it's known as Porthskathow meaning harbour of boats.

PORTLOE

John Betjamin thought Portloe one of the least spoilt and most impressive of Cornish fishing villages and he wasn't mistaken. Portloe in Cornish is Porthlogh meaning cove pool. In the 1890s a local landlord was caught smuggling spirits and hung for his efforts. He was known as 'Black Dunstan' and his much-restructured pub is now part of a notable hotel and spa, the Lugger Hotel. The Walt Disney Corporation chose Portloe to film scenes for their 1950 classic *Treasure Island*. Nearby is Broom Parc House, Veryan, where the 1992 series *The Camomile Lawn* was recorded. Portloe was also used in this television adaptation of Mary Wesley's 1984 novel concerning the eve of World War II in Cornwall. At Veryan there are some very special round houses built by the Reverend Jeremiah Trist in 1820. Two are located at each end of the village and one at the centre, being positioned and built to keep the Devil away and are purposely circular so that Satan couldn't hide in any corners. The unusually designed local church is dedicated to the 5th century St Symphorian.

MEVAGISSEY

Mevagissey has been described as a living Cornish fishing village and is really an amalgamation of two neighbouring settlements named after St Meva and St Issey. Over time the general area was simply referred to as Meva hag Issey, with *hag* simply meaning 'and' in Cornish. It's sometimes nicknamed Porthilly (from Porthhyli meaning saltwater cove in Cornish) and often just called Meva. In Cornish it's known as Lannvorek meaning church site of Morech. It's alleged that the locals hung a monkey in 1805 fearing it was a French Napoleonic spy and because it wouldn't speak in its own defence, deemed guilty by its own silence. The poor creature is nowadays depicted on the town's crest. Mevagissey was the first place in Cornwall to have electric street lamps, with the local Mevagissey Electric Supply Company (est 1895) being imaginatively fuelled by burning pilchard oil. Just like almost everywhere else in Cornwall, the narrow streets were never built for cars, 4x4s or caravans and occasionally some do get stuck... so be warned!

The odour of pilchard cellars and open drains is hardly something to cherish from the olden days, hence the old nickname 'Fishygissey'. The smell and filth probably had an effect on a local farmer's son, Andrew Pears, as around 1788 the young trainee barber left and went off to London. His customers there hated the rough, harsh soaps of the day, which eventually led to him becoming one of the greatest entrepreneurs of the soap making business. He soon perfected an oval shaped soap with a delicate floral perfume and distinctive amber colour. So Pears' soap was born. The Mevagissey Museum (est 1968, free admission) at East Wharf, Inner Harbour, is housed in an old building dating from 1795, once used for constructing and repairing smugglers boats. Mevagissey is a working harbour and the Mevagissey Harbour Aquarium (free admission) is a charitable concern located on the quayside and housed in the old 1897 built RNLI lifeboat house. The small aquarium was established in the mid 1950s and although admission is free all donations are gratefully received. The World of Model Railways (est 1971) is a fun place for enthusiasts and can be tracked down near the harbour in Meadow Street.

The Mevagissey Male Voice Choir is one of the largest choirs in Cornwall, formed in 1974. They raise money for charity and travel all over the world. Deadeye Jack's Cabin (est 2008), located down by the harbour at Oliver's Quay, specialises in pirate souvenirs, toys, gifts and accessories. At Gorran is Caerhays Castle and its magnificent gardens. It was designed by architect John Nash and built in 1810. Mineralogist and clergyman Reverend William Gregor (1761-1817) was born on the nearby Trewarthenick Estate and in 1791 first discovered in the Lizard area a metallic element we now know as titanium. At nearby Pentewan can be found the Lost Gardens of Heligan. In Cornish lost is *koll* (or *kelly*), garden is *jardyn* (or *lowarth*) and Helygen means willow tree. Heligan House was built in 1603 for the Tremayne family, although their descendants eventually rented it out in 1920. The new tenants, the Williamson's were obviously not very keen on gardening and a wilderness soon resulted. Tim Smit and John Nelson met in 1990 with John Willis who had inherited the family pile and the garden's restoration was soon underway with its reclamation shown as a short series of television documentaries in 1996. It's now a tourist must visit site (if it can ever be found!). Tim Smit is also famous as the founder of the Eden Project (see 75).

ST AUSTELL

St Austell is often lovingly referred to as Snozzell and for many years the town's name was written as St Austle. It's known in Cornish as St Austel, being named after the 6th century St Austolus. The town is the largest in Cornwall and is promoted as the gateway to St Austell Bay. Its main claims to fame are the St Austell Brewery, china clay mining (see 12), its proximity to both the world famous Eden Project and the Lost Gardens of Heligan and the fact that actor John Nettles of *Bergerac* and *Midsomer Murders* television fame was born here in 1943. Nowadays St Austell is little more than a modern shopping complex, although within it stands an island of history in the form of Holy Trinity church, dedicated in 1259. Located in Church Street and previously known as St Austolus's church, it has many interesting features including a superb 15th century tower.

The award winning Eden Project with its amazing plants, hotel and futuristic space age looking domes is located at Bodelva, close to St Austell. It occupies 35 acres of the old clay-mining land of Bodelva Pit and first opened in 2001. Its spectacular geodesic biome domes have attracted thousands of visitors ever since. It's an environmental paradise, a global garden and praise indeed must go to Tim Smit, its instigator. The Warm Temperate and Humid Tropics biome domes are marvels of the modern world. In the Rainforest biome, the largest 'captive' (indoor) rainforest in the world, look out for waterfalls and be sure to venture over the aerial treetop walkway and perhaps even the Lookout suspended high up in the dome. Outside, the gardens are spectacular and a free Landtrain can be taken up and down the steep incline to and from the Visitor's Centre. This gem of a site even featured as a diamond mine in the 2002 James Bond epic film *Die Another Day*. Whilst at Eden, lookout for SkyWire soaring overhead. Installed in 2012 and at a length of 2,965 feet, it's the longest zip-wire in Cornwall and indeed in England, affording exhilarating bird's-eye views over the site. The 'flight' slots are bookable... but are not for the faint hearted! An eco-friendly idea at the Eden Project is to tap into the underground 'hot rock' geothermal energy given out by the granite beneath it. The plan is to bore two deep experimental shafts then pump cold water down into one and 'harvest' the resulting steam from the other. As the heat source is endless this could mean the start of Cornwall's answer to cheaper and greener electricity, especially in combination with the ever-increasing output of Cornish solar, wave and wind power.

Cornishman Walter Hicks (1829-1916) established the St Austell Brewery in 1851. It produces around 25 million pints of beer annually and by prior arrangement the brewery runs regular tours from the St Austell Brewery Visitor's Centre in Trevarthian Rd, showing the various stages of the brewing process. There is also an interactive museum, a shop and even a bar where there is a chance to sample their wares. The Rann Wartha Wetherspoon's pub in Biddicks Court (est 2007) gets its name from the Cornish for higher quarter and refers to the local china clay mining area (see 12). In St Austell's Trenance Wood (or Menacuddle Wood) besides the picturesque bank and weir of the St Austell River (near the B3274 Bodmin Road) is located the intriguingly named Menacuddle Holy Well, known for its pure waters and apparent curative powers. The secluded well house dates from the 15th century (restored 1922) and there was a chapel here in 1291 although it has long since gone. The derivation of the name seems to stem from maybe a corruption of St Guidel's sanctuary, perhaps from the Cornish *mena gothall* meaning hillside thicket or from *maen a coedl* meaning hawks stone. It may just simply mean rock well but its healing powers, especially for weak children, were supposedly very strong indeed. A bent pin thrown into the well is meant to bring a long, lucky and healthy life to all that leave them there.

Just outside St Austell is the Wheal Martyn China Clay Heritage Centre (est 1975), part of the Cornish Mining World Heritage Site, which depicts a fascinating insight into china clay mining history. The nearby Treffry Viaduct in the Luxulyan Valley, St Blazey, is an engineering wonder, free to walk across and featured in the 1981 film *Omen III-The Final Conflict*. The viaduct is the masterpiece of Joseph Treffry (1782-1850) and took three years to build. Completed in 1842 it was used to carry water and wagons loaded with copper from the Fowey Consols Mine down to Par Harbour (see 12). North of St Austell lies the village of Roche and the famous Roche Rock outcrop with the ruins of St Michael's chapel at its summit. It has connections with the legends of Jan Tregeagle (see 64) and Tristan and Iseult. Look out for it in the 1981 film *The Final Contact* (*Omen III*). Roche is French for rock, is pronounced 'roach' (like the fish) and is the birthplace of the Cornish comedian Edward Rowe, better known as the 'Kernow King'.

CHARLESTOWN

Charlestown has been described as an historic tall ship harbour and in Cornish is known as Porthmeur meaning great cove. The area was also once known as Polmear and the village of Charlestown as West Polmear. Things changed when wealthy gentleman and entrepreneur Charles Rashleigh (1747-1823) decided on an inspired makeover idea in 1791. By 1801 he had finished building his Georgian town with the aim to export copper, although later china clay became the main commodity though even that stopped being shipped out in 1999. The harbour is rather small and it's a wonder that the tall ships, let alone any of the clay boats, ever managed to negotiate the dog-leg bend in and out of the loading section. It's dominated nowadays by a handful of fully rigged tall ships and it's like being transported back in time to a Cornish harbour of old. The square-riggers and harbour are very popular with film-makers. Such epics as *The Eagle has Landed, Moll Flanders, Frenchman's Creek, The Onedin Line, Poldark, Rebecca, Alice in Wonderland* and even *Dr Who* have all in part been filmed here. The Charlestown Shipwreck & Heritage Centre (est 1976) reinforces the dangers associated with seafarers, in particular its *Titanic* exhibits. Charlestown itself was given World Heritage Status in 2006. An area definitely not part of Charles Rashleigh's plan for Charlestown was Eleven Doors on the opposite side of road to the Rashleigh Arms and further up from the harbour. Nowadays the area is the site of a smart housing estate and the road has been named Eleven Doors in honour of its illustrious past, that being a local haunt for sailors seeking the services of ladies of ill repute. At nearby Par can be found the Wingz Bird Sanctuary, Moorlands Farm, Treesmill, which looks after a variety of birds and animals.

FOWEY

Fowey, a settlement on the River Fowey, has been described as a Cornish dream destination. The Cornish for Fowey is Fowydh, meaning beech river. Fowey is pronounced 'foy', which aptly rhymes with joy. The fortified manor house of the Treffry family was built in 1260 and is known simply as Place, being built on the site of King's (or Kune) Court, a royal palace. Next to Place is the early 14th century church of St Fimbarrus, dedicated to the Irish Saint Finn Barr. Within the church grounds is a granite war memorial erected on the site of the old Rose & Crown Inn, the landlord of which, William Wyatt, was hung for murder at Bodmin in 1811. The Town Quay at the centre of Fowey is a great place to soak up the panoramic harbour views. During the summer Fowey Regatta & Carnival festivities a giant pasty is baked, ferried over the river from nearby Polruan and enjoyed by the attending crowds.

If the Town Quay lies at the centre of Fowey then the sea lies at its very heart. There is always something to catch the eye and boat trips, ferries and self-drive boats are a great way to explore. Trips upstream to see the busy docks and beautiful villages such as Golant, Lerryn, St Winnow and historic Lostwithiel (see 78) are recommended. Fowey Town Tours take passengers from the quay on a sightseeing tour. Both the small Town Museum and the Aquarium (est 1952) are located close to the Town Quay. Local inns include the King of Prussia, the Lugger (1633), the Galleon and, close to St Fimbarrus church, the historic Ship Inn (1570). On the outskirts of Fowey along Polvillion Road near Lankelly Lane is a decorated bus shelter (nearby is a footpath to Readymoney Cove). Sam's Bistro & Lounge (est 1988) in Fore Street is housed in a c1380 merchant's home. Nearby is Noah's Ark, a building dating from pre 1456 and Well House (1430). Antony Hewish was born locally in 1929 and received the Nobel Prize in 1974 for his role in discovering pulsars in 1967, which are highly magnetised, rapidly spinning, neutron stars. At the Foye Old Exchange B&B in Lostwithiel Street there is a fascinating display of old telephones in the window and the owner is Michael Penprase, Fowey town crier (retired).

Fowey Hall was constructed in 1899 for Sir Charles Hanson who was Lord Mayor of London between 1917-1918. Its gatehouse and gateway could well be the inspiration for the wonderful drawing that E. H. Shepard produced for part of Kenneth Grahame's classic

1908 children's story *Wind In The Willows* and it's possibile that Toad Hall itself was actually based on Fowey Hall. There are local connections with Kenneth Grahame as in 1899 he was married in Fowey's St Fimbarrus church, frequently holidayed in the town and often went for local boat trips, all of which inspired his writing. The Fowey Hotel (est 1882) on the esplanade was where Kenneth Grahame wrote letters to his son Alastair containing stories that formed part of *Wind In The Willows*. Fowey hosts the delightful annual Fowey Festival of Words and Music in May, hosted by the du Maurier Festival Society, which celebrates the arts in Fowey with a variety of events staged locally. From the Caffa Mill car park at the Bodinnick car ferry crossing can be seen Ferryside, the former home of Daphne du Maurier (1907-1989). Here she wrote her first novel *The Loving Spirit* (1931), which was based upon the Slade family of Polruan. The original figurehead of the schooner *Jane Slade* can still be seen on the right hand side of the building, just below her old bedroom and was rescued from the muds of Pont Pill where the rotting ship lay abandoned. The steep hill out of Bodinnick leads up to the Hall Walk, a scenic four-mile walk past the point where King Charles I was almost murdered in 1644. It eventually leads round to nearby Polruan. Bodinnick means dwelling by a fort and was once known as Pendennick, with the wonderfully atmospheric Old Ferry Inn well worth visiting.

At the other end of Fowey by the harbour entrance lies Readymoney Cove, the only official beach in Fowey, as the others are fully covered at full tide. Here can be found Point Neptune, a grand old Grade II listed Victorian mansion dating back to the 1860s and built by French prisoners of war, now in the possession of actress, writer and comedien Dawn French. This imposing residence was constructed for William Rashleigh a few years before his death in 1871. He preferred living at Point Neptune to residing in his family home at nearby Menabilly, which was where Daphne du Maurier (1907-1989) later once lived, being Manderley in her famous 1938 story *Rebecca* The nearby Saint's Way (Forth an Syns) footpath is a 30-mile route stretching all the way to Padstow. The stronghold of St Catherine's Castle (free entry) was built in 1540 as part of Henry VIII's coastal defences and was restored in 1855. Not far away along the coast is Polkerris Beach, home to the Polkerris Beach Company, housed in an old 17th century pilchard store and catering for windsurfing, sailing and all such watersports. Also there is the Rashleigh Inn (the 'Inn on the Beach') and Sam's on the Beach restaurant, housed in the old RNLI lifeboat station. In Cornish the village is known as Pollkerys, meaning fortified pool.

Looking across to Polruan, high above the water line and houses, exists a huge buttress, a windowless stump, which is all that remains of St Saviour's Chapel. On the waterline can also be seen an old, square, castle-like building, which is known as the Blockhouse. It was built in about 1380 as a defensive measure after a Spanish attack on the area. There is a similar one on the opposite Fowey side of the harbour, now in ruins and between the two once hung an immense iron chain that could be raised for fortification and lowered into the sea during more peaceful times. Hugging the steep hillside, Polruan is a typically picturesque old fishing and shipbuilding village, which seems to have lost little of its character over the years. Near the 16th century Lugger Inn on the quayside there is the Russell Inn and Crumpets café.

[For more detailed information on the Fowey and Polruan area see: *Fabulous Fowey* by Phil Billington, Polperro Heritage Press (2008)]

LOSTWITHIEL

The ancient town of Lostwithiel has been described in recent years as Cornwall's hidden secret and as the antiques capital of Cornwall. In Cornish it's known as Lostwydhyel meaning tail end of the woodland, or Lestwithiel meaning court or palace of the lion. The concept of Lostwithiel meaning lost within the hills is incorrect. The town was once the administrative capital of Cornwall in the 13th century and also home to the ancient Cornish Stannary Parliament, the Seneth an Stenegow Kernow. Lostwithiel's tin trade gradually dwindled due to progressive silting up of the river and eventually transferred downstream to rival Fowey, situated at the mouth of the estuary. The 13th century Stannary Palace or Old Duchy Palace building (c1292) still exists in part on the corner of Fore Street and Quay Street. Work on the palace began in 1265, being built for Edward, the Black Prince and first Duke of Cornwall, with the design probably based on the Great Hall of Westminster. The remains are of historic importance to Cornwall and, after centuries of slow decay, restoration work finally safeguarded the future of the Exchequer (or Coinage) Hall for the Duchy. In early 2009 it was saved from falling into private hands with aid from Prince Charles's Regeneration Trust in conjunction with the Cornwall Buildings Preservation Trust. Restoration was completed in 2013 and there is now a permanent but modest heritage exhibition housed here. The Globe Inn located in North Street close to the ancient bridge over the River Fowey is steeped in history and both it and the bridge are 13th century structures.

The church of St Bartholomew and the medieval bridge are of great interest, as is the local museum at 16, Fore Street, which is housed in a Georgian building once the local Corn Exchange, partly a gaol and the Guildhall. Cott Road is also the location of the Duchy of Cornwall horticultural nursery. Look out for beers from the local Castle Brewery, especially Lostwithiale! Nearby Restormel Castle is a circular Norman fortress. At nearby St Veep is the church of St Cyrus and St Juliette, which has a rare set of six bells that, when cast in 1770, were found to be perfectly tuned. Not far from Lostwithiel is Lanhydrock House (see 46). Also close by is the privately owned Boconnoc House and Gardens, which has associations with the Pitt family and the famous Pitt Diamond. It's occasionally open to the public for such events as the Cornwall Spring Flower Show, which blossoms in April and a steam fair in July. The original BBC *Poldark* series was in part filmed here.

POLPERRO

Polperro is a typical example of what anyone would think a typical Cornish fishing village should look like. In Cornish it's known as Porthpyra meaning harbour of Pyra. As the River Pol runs through it and *pol* in Cornish means pool, hollow or cove, the village's name may well be derived from cove of Pyra, although some believe it to relate to the pool of the Pyra stream or river. Parking is banned in Polperro during the summer season and visitors can either walk into the centre from the car park, use the mini bus service, or else try an alternate, environmentally friendly mode of transport... electric tram! Polperro used to boast horse-drawn 'buses' that transported people back and forth from the car park down into the heart of the village.

Polperro is a maze of hidden corners, quaint narrow streets and interesting passages, all of which contribute to the magic and old-worldly beauty of the place. Along the Warren over looking the harbour is the Shell House, an old fisherman's cottage completely covered in shells by retired sailor Samuel Puckey. A few fishing boats still work out of Polperro and on the quay is a busy fish market. Close by the harbour wall is a cave known as Willy Willcock's Hole. Apparently he was a fisherman who once disappeared into it, perhaps hiding from the Revenue men, as there are rumours of hidden contraband. His ghost is said to haunt the cave still trying to find a way out. The Crumplehorn Inn located at the top end of the village below the car park was formerly a mill owned by Zephaniah Job (1750-1822), known as the Smugglers' Banker because he masterminded the contraband trade that flourished in Polperro during the latter half of the 18th century. Local fishermen would bring large cargoes of gin, rum, brandy and tobacco back from Guernsey for onward sale ashore and many families prospered from the illegal smuggling trade that was carried on despite the efforts of the Revenue men to put a stop to it. Zephaniah Job's business proved so successful that he even set up one of the first banks in Cornwall, having his own banknotes printed. But the murder of a Customs officer by one of the crew of a Polperro smuggling lugger named the *Lottery* in 1798 led to a manhunt and the eventual arrest of the men responsible; one of them, Tom Potter, was hanged in London. Smuggling declined after that, though still continued for many years.

The Polperro Heritage Museum of Smuggling and Fishing (est 1986) is based in a former pilchard-processing factory in the Warren. It's exhibits graphically tell the story of the smuggling and privateering that once thrived in Polperro and there is an impressive display of local history, photos and memorabilia. All proceeds go towards the upkeep of the harbour. Another interesting old building is Warren Cottage, the birthplace in 1789 of Dr Jonathan Couch (1789-1870), the eminent physician, naturalist and grandfather of author Sir Arthur Quiller-Couch. His illustrated *Fishes of the British Isles*, published in 1864, remains a standard work of reference today. He even had time to write a *History of Polperro*, published shortly after his death in 1870. His whitewashed cottage looks the part of an old Polperro smuggler's dwelling and houses many secret hiding places and even a few hollow walls, as do others. Another building of interest is the 16th century House on Props (or House on Stilts), now a tea room, restaurant and B&B.

The Three Pilchards Inn has a rather steep roof garden, the views from which show just how steep a valley Polperro is situated in. The Polperro Model Village and Land of Legend at the Forge in Mill Hill, has been entertaining visitors for over 60 years and even has a model railway. Chapel Pool is a local bathing spot that's a dream of an infinity tidal pool and as for paddling, Maids Pool is just ideal. Near the Blue Peter Inn is a bench dedicated to the memory of Eva Cloke, placed there by the Polperro Fisherman's Choir, which she co-founded in 1923. In June when Polperro has a midsummer festival, one of the highlights is the mock election of a mayor who, along with a merry entourage, travels around the village handing out fake banknotes and thoroughly testing the quality of beer available. At the end of all this merriment the 'mayor' is subjected to an unceremonious ducking in the waters of the harbour.

LOOE

Looe is the former shark fishing capital of Cornwall and its name derives from its Cornish name Logh, meaning deep pool or inlet. It was originally two villages, East Looe, which was once known as Loo (or Looe) and West Looe, which was once Port Bigham. West and East Looe eventually joined forces in 1883 and became simply Looe. The Victorians in their infinite wisdom demolished a 13-arch, stone bridge, built in 1436, and replaced it in 1854 with the one that exists today. The old stone bridge had a chapel in the middle dedicated to St Anne. The Victorians really loved Looe and called it the 'playground of Plymouth'. It's Cornwall's second largest fishing port. The main shopping street and the waterside run parallel to each other yet seem like two totally different worlds. In the days of the pilchard fleets it would have been heaving with boats and fishermen and was far busier than it is nowadays. It's the old, authentic quarter of Looe, indeed at its very heart and soul, unlike the more tourist-based parts. The Jolly Sailor Inn in West Looe is affectionately known locally as the Jolly and is one of the oldest pubs in the country, being established in 1516. It was once the local haunt of the Atkins sisters who owned Looe Island for many years. In 1964 Babs and Evelyn bought two cottages in Looe with the idea of turning one of them into a working pottery but they also fell in love with Looe Island, also known as St George's Island, that lies half a mile offshore. It's an old smugglers' haunt and in World War II the Germans actually bombed it thinking it was a battleship! The two sisters bought it in 1965, for what seems like a give-away price now of £22,000 for the 22-acre island. Babs wrote two books about their trials and tribulations both on and off it, namely *We Bought an Island* (1976) and its sequel *Tales from our Cornish Island* (1986). Evelyn died at the age of 87 in 1997 and Babs in 2004, aged 86 and the island was bequeathed to the Cornwall Wildlife Trust, who manage it as a marine nature reserve. Boat trips round the island and even ones onto it are very popular and can be booked at East Looe harbour.

In comparison to quiet West Looe, East Looe is full of shops, has a family orientated beach and the feel of a holiday resort. The 2008 ITV series *Echo Beach* was filmed and based in East Looe, although it was re-named Polnarren. On the West Looe side of the harbour is a bronze statue (2008) by sculptor Suzie Marsh of a one-eyed grey seal named Nelson who was once a regular visitor and a great favourite with all. In the 15th century Guildhall and Gaol building in Higher Market Street is housed the Old Guildhall Museum (est 1972), featuring an exhibition of Looe's history from the Domesday Book right up to the present day, including smuggling, fishing and even their own resident ghost.

Smuggler's Cottage, now a restaurant, was built around 1430 and was once a smuggler's haunt supposedly having tunnels and passages leading down to the harbour. When it was restored in 1595 lots of old beams and timbers that had been salvaged from the Spanish Armada were used. Other buildings of interest are the Golden Guinea restaurant (1632) and J M Bray & Son whose shop was built in 1666, the same year as the Great Fire of London. In 1837 a very lucky man named Davies Gilbert inherited a house in Fore Street from the late town clerk. In a cupboard there he found a stash of £10,000 in solid gold guineas, an immense fortune in those days and all in cash! An intriguing one-handed 18th century turret clock was given to St Mary's church (located in Higher Chapel Street) by Edward Trelawny in 1737 and was restored by public subscriptions in 1996. Ye Olde Fisherman's Arms in Higher Market Street is a 16th century beamed, atmospheric inn, as is Ye Olde Salutation Inn in Fore Street, the ground floor of which slopes slightly to allow any floodwaters that come in to flow out again through the opposite door. The inn also has dozens of photos of old Looe and of sharks with whoever caught them. Nowadays they are caught, tagged and released, so there are no more dead exhibits on the quayside. There's a move afoot to ban even tagging them and just let people go shark watching. The biennial Looe Lugger Regatta attracts a large number of old sailing vessels whenever it takes place. A special railway journey from Looe to Liskeard is known as the Looe Valley Line and along its scenic nine miles of track a Real Ale Trail has been instigated. Not far from Looe is the Wild Futures Monkey Sanctuary (formally Looe Monkey Sanctuary) at Murrayton House, St Martins. It was established in 1964 by Len Williams and is home to a colony of Amazonian woolly monkeys. At Trecangate is located the Porfell Wildlife Park and Sanctuary.

LISKEARD

The old stannary town of Liskeard means fortified place. It has been known as Liscarret and in Cornish is Lyskerrys, meaning court or seat of justice of the local chief or king. Entry to the Liskeard and District Museum (est 2002) at Foresters Hall, Pike Street, is free, as it is to St Martin's church, the second largest in Cornwall. Well worth viewing is the mural in Pigmeadow Lane depicting historic events of the area. The scenic Looe Valley Line Railway runs nine miles between Looe and Liskeard railway station, located at Grove Park Court, just off Station Road. Pipewell (Pipe Well) located in Well Lane is fed from four springs, has apparently never run dry and is said to possess special healing powers and lucky effects with matrimony. By the library in Barras Street can be found Stuart House where in 1644 Charles I lodged during the Civil War. The Adrenalin Quarry (est 2009) is located on Lower Clicker Road near Menheniot, just off the A38 and boasts one of the UK's longest zip wires, a 'flying' experience in Hoverworld, a giant swing and much more. A great day out but certainly not for the faint-hearted!

PORTWRINKLE

Portwrinkle is known in Cornish as Porthwykkel, which possibly means cove of the hidden or secret water. It's an isolated place described as being located in the forgotten corner of Cornwall. Of special interest is the entirely man-made 15 feet deep and seven foot high Sharrow Grotto cave in the cliffs, completed in 1784 by James Lugger. The very act of doing so apparently cured his gout and he left a carved inscription on the grotto wall to commemorate his tunnelling achievement. Nearby Crafthole (Craft Hole) is known in Cornish as Skianztoll, which possibly means cave/hole of wisdom and is the location of a curiously named 15th century coaching inn. Finnygook Inn is so called after Silas Finny, a local 18th century smuggler who argued with his fellow villains and turned informer on them. He was murdered at nearby Bligers Well for his betrayal and his restless ghost is said to haunt the area. At Rame Head is an old disused World War II lookout post and RAF Radar Station. In Cornish Rame is known as Penn (or Hordh).

Nearby Kingsand, until 1844, was actually part of Devon but thankfully it's now part of Cornwall, as its twin village of Cawsand has always been. The port of Cremyll lies on the edge of Plymouth Sound and the historic Mount Edgcumbe Estate with its 1547 built Tudor mansion house is worth seeing. The origins of the ferry over the River Tamar estuary date back to at least the 8th century and there are written records of its existence in 1204. The journey over to Plymouth, Devon, is about a 15-minute trip. In nearby Torpoint is Anthony House, a private mansion built between 1711 and 1721. Walt Disney's film *Alice in Wonderland* (2010) starring Johnny Depp was partly shot here and the gardens are open to the public as is, more infrequently, the house.

SALTASH

Saltash is deemed the gateway to Cornwall and the name literally means salt mill by the ash tree. It was once just known as Ash and in Cornish is known as Essa. By the waterside in Tamar Street, under the shadow of the railway bridge, is the prominent Union Inn, painted as a giant Union Jack flag and having murals on its side depicting all things local. There is even a statue nearby of Isambard Kingdom Brunel (1806-1859) himself, lovingly guarding his masterpiece. The pub was specially painted in 1994 in celebration of the 50th anniversary of the World War II D-Day Normandy landings in France 1944 and has remained like it ever since! Saltash's other claim to fame is Mary Newman. She was Sir Francis Drake's first wife, with the couple marrying in 1569 at nearby St Budeaux church in Devon. Mary was apparently born in Saltash, although there are doubts about this claim. Her quaint 15th century cottage in Culver Road, if indeed it was hers, is open to the public and was built c1480. Along Fore Street look out for the 'talking seat', which is a bench with a life-sized model of famous River Tamar ferrywoman and gig-rower Ann Glanville (1796-1880) seated on it. Port Eliot House and Gardens are located at nearby St Germans but viewing is restricted so check beforehand. St Germans was named after St Germanus and the present church (consecrated 1261) replaced one established by the saint himself in AD 430, which between then and 1042 was the cathedral for Cornwall. Other places worth visiting include Cotehele, a 13th century medieval house with mill at St Dominick; the nearby 11th century motte and bailey Trematon Castle and the Georgian Trematon Manor. At St Ann's Chapel in Gunnislake is the Tamar Valley Donkey Park, home to the Tamar Donkey Sanctuary, where you can even adopt a donkey.

Isambard Kingdom Brunel's famous Royal Albert Bridge here at Saltash is a sheer joy to behold. He was chief designer and engineer on the project and by 1855 the River Tamar was his to tame. The job was completed by 1859 and it was opened by Prince Albert. The bridge's height is sufficient enough to clear an old man-of-war ship with all her canvas set, a very important requirement at the time. An enormous Celtic cross designed by Fowey sculptor Simon Thomas was painstakingly installed in Elwell Wood beside the Tamar Road Bridge in 2013. The impressive carbon fibre cross stands over 65 feet tall, with its gold, silver and copper colours reflecting Cornwall's mining heritage. This iconic gateway landmark symbolically welcomes one and all into the glorious Duchy of Cornwall.

CORNWALL<CORNWALL>CORNWALL
KERNOW<KERNOW~KERNOW>KERNOW

****

This completes the Guidebook section (1-83) of this Standard English Language (SEL) version Passport Book. Please note further travel documentation may be required upon the future implementation of visa/entry permit certification

In the event of a damaged, destroyed, stolen or lost passport, replace immediately.

DO **NOT** TRAVEL WITHOUT A VALID PASSPORT

***

KERNOW<KERNOW~KERNOW>KERNOW